One Foot on the Floor

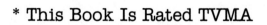

One Foot on the Floor

The Curious Evolution of Sex on Television from *I Love Lucy* to *South Park*

LOUIS CHUNOVIC

New York

Library of Congress Cataloging-in-Publication Data
Chunovic, Louis.
    One foot on the floor : the curious evolution of sex on television from "I Love Lucy" to
    "South Park" / by Louis Chunovic.
        p. c.m.
    Includes bibliographical references and index.
    ISBN 1-57500-186-1
    1. Television programs—United States—Plots, themes, etc. 2. Sex on television. I. Title.
    PN1992.3.U5 C44 2000
    791.45'6538—dc21

                                                                        99-059114

The publisher has made every effort to secure permission to reproduce copyrighted material and would like to apologize should there have been any errors or omissions.

TV Books, L.L.C.
1619 Broadway, Ninth Floor
New York, NY 10019
www.tvbooks.com

Interior design by Rachel Reiss.
Manufactured in the United States of America.

As the novelty of television wears off, the lure of the sexy and the macabre also wears thin.

Christian Century magazine, an editorial, May 28, 1952

for Leslie

Contents

Acknowledgments

MY THANKS TO PETER KAUFMAN, PRESIDENT OF TV BOOKS, WHO brought this project to me, and to Albert DePetrillo, associate editor, who made it his mission to see it done right.

My thanks, too, to Ned Comstock, gifted and generous librarian at the Cinema-TV Library at the University of Southern California, and to So Young Park, the very model of pleasant professionalism at the Arts & Entertainment Network.

Thanks as well to Anne Tschida, my preferred authority on local history and mores in places as diverse as Miami, Hong Kong, and Berlin; and to Jane Thalken, for her encyclopedic recall, particularly about the more obscure bits of sex on television.

And to Doc Feiler: a special thanks for the customary consultations.

The Author's Apologia

FIRST COME THE COURTSHIP RITUALS, THEN COMES THE MAR-
riage, then the babies. This progression, or some less genteel variation of it, is what we all learned in school, or at least from
television. But what about the sex? In the "real" world of the present day, surely the ratio of sex acts to subsequent weddings and
eventual births is huge. A couple hundred couplings for each exchange of vows? A few thousand for each newborn?

But that's hardly the way it's been on television, at least not as
it started out. On TV, new family units formed and little babies
came into existence, sometimes even growing up before our
eyes to become Little Ricky (Ricardo) or big Rick (Nelson or
Schroder, take your pick), but it was all ex nihilo, as it were.
"Rogering" or the "Beast With Two Backs," as the Bard himself—with a wink and a nudge to rollicking Elizabethan audiences—used to call it, was deemed a subject unfit for the great
American viewing public.

Back in those black and white days the love that dared not
speak its name on television was spelled S-E-X. But that was way
back in the first decades of the second half of the twentieth century, when finding some trace of "it" on the tube was about as un-

likely as, say, a public discussion of a semen stain on a certain little blue Gap dress.

And now? Belly buttons are okay, plunging necklines are certainly okay, as are teeny-tiny bikinis. Want to make something of
it, a joke perhaps? If "dumb stick" and "trouser dowser" don't do
it for you, perhaps you want to say "penis" on TV? Go right
ahead, kid. How about getting on television and pronouncing that
you'll soon be kicking some butt face's ass? Sure, but only right-
eously or, better yet, just metaphorically. Meaningless raunch is in,
meaningless violence is out. And that's the way it is at the beginning of the twenty-first century!

Some fervent guardian of early fifties TV morality, a publicity-
seeking congressman perhaps, would be shocked right down to
his argyle socks to see how freely the Beast With Two Backs stalks
today's prime time. And today's ratio of TV sex acts to TV weddings and TV babies? Astronomical!

NETWORK TELEVISION HAS ALWAYS BEEN A MANSION WITH MANY
rooms—a department store, as the late Brandon Tartikoff, the
master programmer of the 1980s, characterized it, and that was especially so in the Three Network days of the monolithic mass audience. In fact, so big is the world of TV that on some level of
close analysis, the *opposite* of almost every proposition you can
make about the tube turns out also to be true; which is to say, for
every *All in the Family* there is also a *Brady Bunch.* But especially if
you look with the benefit of hindsight, even the wholesome
Bunch, with its closeted gay "father" and incest-minded "kids," dissolves into something truly weird. But that kind of analysis is for
another book. Here, it's not the *Brady Bunch* or even *Love American
Style,* but *All in the Family* that your humble author deems the
more significant in the great history of sex on television.

So here, gentle reader, you will find many of the shows and many of the moments that raised the temperature of television.

What qualifies a show or a moment for inclusion in the great pageant? True, the bar of qualifications does tend to fluctuate up and down. Some moments, such as those harmonic convergences when bickering series stars finally "get together" (as they did in *M*A*S*H, Cheers, Moonlighting,* and others), mean something only to the regular fans who were watching and following along.

But many other moments and series either say something important about the country at a particular time (for example, *Miami Vice* in the 1980s), or they meant something *to* the country at large at a particular time. In the 1970s, for example, *All in the Family* arguably affected the national discourse about bigotry, the war in Southeast Asia, and a host of other issues. And that's why you'll find Elvis on *The Ed Sullivan Show* in the mid-fifties. After all, why do you think all those teary-eyed, damp, teenage girls were screaming and jumping around?

And there's this, too, to ponder: Hit shows tend to go on and on and on, sometimes for a decade and more, so a history that discusses them in any detail will have to occasionally abandon its orderly chronological progression. Take *Roseanne,* for example. Did that series have more of an impact when it debuted in the late eighties, trashing the oh-so-tidy upper-middle class monopoly on sitcom lives, or when its star did public battle with the network in the mid-nineties over the issue of including a "lesbian kiss" in one episode?

So of necessity expect to find a modest cognitive dissonance in these pages, of the kind you might experience while banging channels on your own remote. Think of it as the digression of a stubbornly nonlinear sensibility, if you'd like, and pay it no further mind.

And, finally, there's this: After more than half a century of broadcasts—by stations, by networks (broadcast and cable), by groups and syndicators—the universe of television is so vast and various that *any* analysis of the history and highlights of sex on TV, such as the one you will find here, is of necessity subjective and selective.

So to those whose favorite flickering moment, possibly even a treasured pre-pubescent memory, has been overlooked, I apologize in advance.

The Biz

What It Was, How It Is

WHEN FORMER UNITED STATES SENATOR DALE BUMPERS EXplained, "H. L. Mencken one time said, 'When you hear somebody say, "This is not about money," it's about money. And when you hear somebody say "This is not about sex," it's about sex,'" he was not talking about TV. But when he made those famous, folksy (and of course televised) remarks in the well of the U.S. Senate on Thursday, January 21, 1999, he might as well have been.

Money? Sex? TV?! Of course.

The medium of broadcast television, jaded and cynical insiders will be delighted to tell you, historically has *not* been in the business of delivering entertainment to audiences. Instead, it has been, and for the most part still is, in the business of delivering those audiences to the advertisers who pay (very big) money for the privilege of having an in-home forum from which to hawk their wares. And of course, we've known since Sophocles at least that there's no better audience grabber than sex.

But from its earliest beginnings in the late 1940s, TV has faced a conundrum: How to rivet that mass audience the advertisers covet without at the same time offending important segments of it? This was especially important in the first four decades of the medium when that audience was national and monolithic, and everyone—young or old, sophisticated or naive, devout or not—was watching the very same programs at the very same time.

Pssst, hey kids. Heard the one about the traveling sales-man, the farmer's daughter, and the broadcasters' association?

No? Well, gather 'round the flickering cathode-ray tube, boys and girls, and remember back to when leggy cigarette packs danced across the console Motorola, when Lucky Strike meant fine tobacco, and nine out of ten doctors (as well as such distinguished TV thespians as *Death Valley Days* host Ronald Reagan) touted the health benefits and swell social pleasures of cigarette smoking.

America was different then. It was a country of conformity as visible as the suburban tract homes going up all around the land. The generation that grew up in the Great Depression and fought and won World War Two wanted peace and prosperity. Their kids—the Boomers—growing up watching TV and listening to AM rock and roll on the family car radio, wanted it ecstatic and real. And the advertisers in those far-off days wanted to reach the biggest audience possible.

The new medium enthusiastically advertised cigarettes and alcohol and big, beautiful new cars to get from the dreary old cities to all those new appliance-equipped homes in the sunny suburbs, where happy nuclear families with apple-cheeked young children were basking in the material pleasures of washers and dryers and frost-free refrigerators and . . . your very own black-and-white TV!

Getting and spending, after the Great Depression and the years of World War Two hardship, was all the rage. The young men recently returned from the war and moving into those suburbs with their sweethearts were in no mood for more risk-taking. Understandably, they were more interested in peace and order, and domestic tranquility, and they were intent on their legacy—raising all those young children of the vast Baby Boom generation who grew up in tandem with the medium of television.

Those very first TV viewers could settle back on their couches and tune in to a new show called *Candid Microphone,* which specialized in funny and mostly innocent tricks on unsuspecting participants, pranks like the typewriter that spewed its paper back at a would-be secretary, or the talking mailbox, or the bowling ball without finger holes. Originally created for radio by a young WW II vet named Allen Funt, a year after its 1948 debut the show was renamed *Candid Camera.* At first, hiding those bulky early television cameras, the size of refrigerators, was the show's toughest challenge, but as the years went by technology took care of that problem. Did anyone watching then have any idea of where it would all lead a half century later?

The beginning of the medium coincided with the first *Kinsey Report* on human sexuality in 1948. It also coincided with the start of a grand grudge match, as bone-crunching as the professional wrestling spectacles so popular in the first days of television: the free world versus the evil empire! This was also known as the Cold War.

As TV began in America, McCarthyism—the inquisitorial pursuit of hidden "godless" Communists in government and Hollywood and the uprooting of other un-American and immoral enemies—was on the march. While an influential publication called *Red Channels* was exposing erstwhile Communists in Hollywood (and ruining many a career in the process), the same self-appointed guardians that protected American values against the

Red Menace were also ever-vigilant against other, homegrown deviations from the straight-and-narrow American Way. And the critics and crusaders and vigilantes had to look no further than that compelling new box, glowing in the living room corner.

In those earliest days, most TV shows were done live, and live TV meant the excitement of uncertainty, which included the occasional falling shoulder strap or verbal slip or even a "blue" joke, sometimes even on children's television.

"What's the difference between a snow woman and a snow man?" a manic comic asked on a kid's show once in those live broadcasting days. The answer he reportedly gave, "Snow balls!," got him thrown off the air.

CONGRESSMEN, THUNDERING THEIR SHOCK AND DISMAY OVER A handful of well-publicized miscues in the early fifties, prepared to probe the moral standards of broadcasting, even while powerful private watchdog groups, like the influential Catholic Legion of Decency, "approved" (or banned) movies and threatened to do the same with TV.

After all, even in flickering, snowy black and white it was patently obvious that the medium had a new and unprecedented power—to make a career, to ignite a trend, to affect the entire country at a single stroke—and the pols and the priests and the other guardians of the public welfare and morality understood it at once.

And it was just as obvious that owning one of the new television stations sprouting up around the country would be like having a license to print money. And furthermore, the right to broadcast on a particular *publicly owned* frequency, granted by the government to each and every individual station, also conceivably could be taken away. In those early years of television, in that atmosphere of fear and political witch hunt, and well before the era of civil rights and the women's and gay rights movements, civil libertarians and others had little chance of opposing the would-be censors.

At first, any mention at all of sex on TV was strictly taboo— so much so that the ubiquitous censors mandated that even married couples portrayed on the new medium must sleep in separate beds, and the very word "pregnant" was banned from the airwaves.

It was in the darkening atmosphere of late 1951 that the brand new National Association of Radio and Television Broadcasters, representing America's 108 television stations and fearful of imminent government "intervention," came up with its own proposal for a voluntary good-conduct Code of Ethics. That code banned, among other things, jokes about traveling salesmen and farmers' daughters, as well as "such views of performers as emphasize anatomical details indecently." The broadcasters also warned their membership that the "use of locations closely associated with sexual life or with sexual sin must be governed by good taste and delicacy."[1]

Good taste and delicacy?

Most societies have had their censorious segments and upright citizens' brigades, those intent on upholding standards and mandating good taste and delicacy for the benighted masses. Take, for just one example, the late Victorians of Great Britain, which was then the world's super power. They knew a thing or two about the varieties of pleasure, too, but they had their Obscene Publications Act as well, zealously enforced by such influential private groups as the Society for the Suppression of Vice.

Now, flash forward to the present day. Present-day TV has its code, too, and even a ubiquitous ratings system, warning the viewers (and their parents) about everything from vice to violence to bad language.

"OH, MY GOD! MY NIPPLE'S PIERCED!" THE BRUSHCUT, STRAIGHT-arrow, ex-Navy Seal hired by a recalcitrant magazine publisher to be his private fitness trainer, has just peered down into his open shirt. Looking again, more closely, he cries out in horror: "Where does that chain go?!"

It's just another Thursday night of TV on the cusp of the new millennium, and the badly hungover former commando is a passing character on *Just Shoot Me*, the primetime NBC sitcom about life at a *Cosmo*-like magazine. He's been out all night, on a date with the aptly named Nina Van Horn (Wendie Malick), a sex-obsessed, pill-popping, X-ray-thin former model with a comical taste for B&D. Nina breezes into the scene, zinging quips as always, and asks the ex-Seal his name.

"Noodleman," he groans.

She gapes at him, wide-eyed and with mock innocence. "That used to be *my* name," she proclaims. "We're cousins!"

Present-day primetime *broadcast network* TV doesn't stop at just talking about mammary protuberances either. A little later that same season, NBC aired *Cleopatra,* a two-part miniseries about the seductress of the Nile. Did more viewers tune in for the quasi-historical spectacle, or for the heavily hyped diaphanous costumes, such as the one that clearly revealed the sultry Egyptian queen's nipples?

Another night, another network: On ABC, in an episode of *The Norm Show,* a sitcom set in a social-welfare office, the perpetually sheepish title character (Norm Macdonald) admits that he's violated the primary rule of social workers by sleeping with a client. But she turns out to have just a touch of nymphomania, so it's all right. Three of the four sitcoms on ABC that Wednesday night, in fact, have plots drenched with innuendo (and more) about sex.

Click. On a Monday night, over at Fox Broadcasting, the so-called Fourth Network, the droll and satirical *Ally McBeal* unspools a plot that finds two of its reliably randy characters, Billy (Gil Bellows) and Georgia (Courtney Thorne-Smith), a married couple at Cage/Fish & Associates, the show's ultra-trendy Boston law firm, reigniting their romance by having sex inside a stall in the firm's famous unisex bathroom. Meanwhile, the unabashedly incorrect and politically unreconstructed Richard Fish (Greg Germann) ends up in bed for the first time with the sexually aggressive and matter-of-factly imperious Ling Woo (Lucy Liu), also aptly named.

"This is an E-ticket, Richard," Ling whispers breathily into Richard's ear when he slips into bed next to her. She moves even closer, reaching under the covers, clearly groping below Richard's waist, and murmurs the punchline: "With a minimum size requirement to ride."

But before the fun can start, Ling whips out a waiver ("It says you have no known heart conditions, no history of seizures, no back injuries") and a confidentiality agreement ("I have trade secrets," Ling purrs) for a boggled Richard to sign. Under the pressure to perform ("Action!" Ling shouts, leaping on him), Richard deflates, so the thwarted duo settles down in bed to—what else?—watch TV. The show that's on, *Chicago Hope,* is an "in" joke, too. It's produced by David E. Kelley, *Ally*'s creator.

Fade out, fade in. Richard is at the doctor's office, learning that the unnamed performance pill he's getting a prescription for (clearly, it's Viagra) "does not produce spontaneous erections. It must be accompanied by a sexual stimulus." For Ling, reclining in her bedroom at the end of the episode, a sexual stimulus is just what the sight of the pharmaceutically aroused Richard is. To the pulsing R&B sound of "I'm Just a Love Machine," Richard, wearing only a silk robe, leaps up on the foot of her bed. As Ling writhes below, we view her astounded face in a camera angle that gives us a vantage point from behind and below Richard's robe and through his bare legs. *Ooooh, baby,* the off-screen singers harmonize, as Richard drops his robe and Ling, transported, strains upward.

IN TV-LAND, WHERE TWO OF ANYTHING QUALIFIES AS A TREND, Viagra, the anti-impotence drug, seemed to be the plot device of choice for sitcoms and one-hour networks dramas alike as the last TV season of the second millennium drew to a close. A few seasons before, the big trend was the "lesbian kiss." *Roseanne* and *Ellen* both had heavily hyped episodes that included the promotably titillating sapphic osculation.

But the sight of two men kissing on TV remained exceeding rare. By the late nineties, *Will & Grace,* a show about a gay man sharing an apartment with a straight woman, was ensconced on the NBC schedule. Like many other sitcoms on the Peacock Network it was ribald, witty, and suggestive. But, as the critics remarked, nowhere in its first season was there any indication that either Will, the titular gay man, or Jack, his extravagantly effete friend, was having sex in any manner whatsoever, not even a kiss with another man. On the other hand, *That '70s Show,* on the relatively more daring Fox network, did have a gay kiss moment that passed without any critical notice at all. In it, naive Wisconsin teen Eric becomes pals with handsome Buddy, a rich kid with a red Trans Am. They're sitting in his car, Eric is yammering away, and Buddy plants one right on his mouth. Eric is stunned into silent disbelief.

Later on, just in time for the February 2000 sweeps, *Will &
Grace* did break the two-gay-men-kissing barrier with a clever
episode in which Will and Jack protest the *lack* of a gay kiss on an
NBC sitcom by kissing on live TV, on the street in front of the
Today show window. Two men smooching in prime time it may
have been, witty commentary it may have been, but the kiss itself
was presented in an entirely unsexual context.

Not only were the *McBeal* regulars gamboling thanks to Viagra,
but series as dissimilar as *Law and Order* and *Melrose Place* aired
episodes in which characters died overdosing on a Viagra-like
drug. In fact, in one of the last *Melrose* episodes before the long-
running camp classic went off the air, silver-haired Tony died
while having sex with Lexi, who'd just convinced him to sign a
contract by reposing naked on a bed, "wearing," like some papyrus
bikini, only the document's three pages. Actually, death after sex is
a time-honored tradition in primetime soaps. During a 1981
episode of *Dynasty*, Cecil Colby (Lloyd Bochner) died for his orgasm when sex with the scheming Alexis (Joan Collins) ended
with a fatal heart attack.

And that's just how it is in broadcast-network prime-time, the
kind of over-the-air television anyone with a set can get. Perhaps
you'd rather try basic cable, to which some two-thirds of us now
have access, on a random week night, just after prime time.

Click. On E! Entertainment Television, Howard Stern is
spreading mayonnaise on the exposed posterior cheeks of a
woman in a bikini who is bent over, hands on knees, with her
backside thrust up at the camera. When he's done slathering on
the mayo, Howard and a crony start flinging bologna at the
woman's mayonnaise-covered bottom.

Click. Same time, another channel: On FX, Fox's cable network, on the new *The X Show*, three self-proclaimed surfer

chicks, model-pretty Southern California blondes, are in a contest to see who can wiggle out of her bra, top, and shorts and get
into a bikini first—just as she might do under a towel on a
crowded beach, an announcer says. But this is on air, so one young
woman simply turns away from the camera and takes off her top.
The winning "chick" gets a surfboard—as well as soaked when a
bucket of water is upended over her head.

HOW DID WE GET TO HERE FROM THERE IN THE SPACE OF
a single boggled viewer's lifetime?

How did we get from Lucy in the 1950s' most popular TV sitcom, forbidden to say the word "pregnant," to Phoebe in *Friends*
blithering brightly about implanting an embryo in her uterus so
she can bear an infertile couple's child? Even the Parents Television Council, a conservative standard-bearer dedicated to monitoring language, sex, and violence on TV, and to bringing back the
once-sacrosanct concept of "family hour" programming, has
given up tallying such words as "hell," "damn," and "butt" for its
index of "foul" TV language, because, in everyday life, those words
have simply become too pervasive.[2]

Are we, as a society, so much more sophisticated now than in
the early 1950s, when broadcasters were promising solemnly to
outlaw "profanity, obscenity, smut, and vulgarity," as well as "camera angles that emphasize anatomical details indecently"?[3]

For decades, those promises were enforced by censors, hired
by the broadcasters themselves. The truth is that then, as now, TV
censorship was largely a voluntary matter, its application mostly
matter-of-fact and sometime maddeningly capricious. Then networks and media began to proliferate. Increased competition for
the advertising dollar could always be counted on to trump all
other considerations, and eventually, in the late 1970s, when

cable and VCRs began to crowd in, competition overtook principle and the censors, just like the Evil Empire itself, simply faded away.

So how did we get here? Let's review the tape (and the kinescope).

MID-TWENTIETH-CENTURY CONGRESSIONAL SABER-RATTLING WAS partly disarmed by the broadcasting trade association's own first Code of Ethics. As critics on both sides of the question realized right from the beginning, the code was designed (perhaps *had* to be designed) to be unenforceable.

And that was because, right from the beginning, there was simply too much TV being aired for any single group of censors to view. The first code called for a review board to maintain a "continuing review" of all programming. That board had just five members.

So then, how to account for censorship's effectiveness? For one thing, the board could set standards and hear complaints; for another, there was also censorship courtesy of the almighty advertiser.

In the beginning of TV, advertisers wielded enormous power over programming. They owned programs and even time periods outright, and representatives of the biggest advertisers and their agencies sometimes maintained their own offices right on the studio lots, from where they could take their red pencils to scripts while they were still in development.

That grip wasn't loosened at all until the 1960s, when the networks innovated a practice called "scatter buying," which allowed an advertiser to put dollars into commercial "time" throughout the network's schedule and had the side effect of lessening the impact of any one advertiser on any single program. In our more enlightened present day, with scores and scores of networks "narrowcasting" to small, specific audience segments, that trend is once again reversing, with advertisers regaining creative control over entire programs and time periods.

But back in TV's early days, not alienating competing audience segments could quickly veer into absurdity. That was demonstrated at one early fifties Washington hearing by no less than the chairman of the subcommittee charged with the first investigation of broadcasting morality. As the honorable congressman from Arkansas, Ezekiel Candler Gathers, explained, complaining publicly about one offensive program, "It had a grass-skirted young lady and a thinly clad gentleman dancing the hootchy-kootchy. They danced to a very lively tune and shook the shimmy, both of them. And it ended by the very attractive young lady shaking all the way down to the floor, landing on her hands, with a gentleman standing close by. My children saw that and I could not get it turned off to save my life. I tried."[4]

Right, E. C., you tried.

The Fifties

Plunging Necklines, Lucy, and the King of Rock and Roll

The costuming of all performers shall be within the bounds of propriety and shall avoid such exposure or such anatomical detail as would embarrass or offend home viewers.

The use of locations closely associated with sexual life or with sexual sin must be governed by good taste and delicacy....

Illicit sex relations are not treated as commendable.

Sex crimes and abnormalities are not treated as commendable.

The exposition of sex crimes will be avoided.

—From the first Code of Television Standards,
National Association of Radio and Television
Broadcasters,
March 1951

IN THE 1950S THE CENSORS DID TRY, REPEATEDLY AND VO-ciferously, to condemn the immorality of the glamorous young women (starlets, we learned to call them: models and actresses) who dared appear on variety and panel shows wearing the same kind of glamorous, low-cut gowns they would slip into for an evening at a nightclub, a place to see and be seen, say, Ciro's in L.A. or "21" in New York. (Formal dress for both women and men on talk and variety programs was practically mandatory in the medium's earliest days; after all, the thinking went, the performers were guests in the viewers' living rooms.)

These young beauties became the very first stars to come out of TV itself, sometimes just by riding the wave of censorious publicity; they were women like Faye Emerson, a one-time film actress, known both for being married to a son of the late President Franklin Roosevelt and for the dresses she wore on her own talk show.

The singular victory of the Gathers subcommittee was its successful crusade to raise those "plunging necklines." That crusade had been spurred particularly by the televised décolletage of Dagmar, another tall (5′9″), buxom (40″), young (twenty-three-year-old) TV actress and quiz-show panelist of the period, who became a national wonderment in 1950 solely by virtue of appearing on the new medium.

Reciting doggerel in an untrained voice or just sitting cutely on the sidelines, clearly bored, her ample chest heaving, she was TV's first incarnation of the airily clueless showgirl, which is a close approximation of what Dagmar actually had been before her big break. In the Broadway chorus from which she'd been plucked, she had gone by "Jennie Lewis," but her real name was Virginia Ruth Egnor.

Jerry Lester, then a famous comic, had the brainstorm of hiring her for his late-night NBC talk and variety show, *Broadway Open House,* which was television's original national late-night show. He even came up with the idea of the Dagmar name. Of her debut, Dagmar said, "All I had to do was bring a sexy evening gown, so I got out my royal blue velvet with the white ermine on top and got right over to the studio. There was no script or anything. They said, 'You just sit there and act dumb. Your name is Dagmar.'"[5]

Although she was billed as a singer with Milton DeLugg's quintet, for the first several months Dagmar never sang a note. Her actual job was just to wear those spectacular strapless evening gowns and view the proceedings, usually with an exquisitely bored (some said, vapid) look on her face, from the vantage point of a stool set up near the band. Eventually, as her popularity soared to some five hundred fan letters per week, she was allowed to leave her perch to read a poem or a monologue in the innocent, untutored voice that turned every sentence into a question.[6]

None of that mattered. Dagmar became the first single-named celebrity of the TV era. Just a dimpled Kewpie doll in a low-cut dress, she went in the space of a few months from $25 a week to $1250, with competing networks throwing thousands more at her to do her own show, and toy companies vying for the right to make a Dagmar doll. She was a sensation with the panting male population, as well as a pinup for the soldiers fighting in Korea.

She was the new medium's own "It Girl," but she wasn't the only one. In TV's earliest years, when broadcasts were generally live, those plunging necklines occasionally plunged even farther than expected, baring a nipple or even an entire breast on national television. Faye Emerson on her talk show; all-girl band leader Ina Ray Hutton on her variety show; buxom fifties starlet Jayne Mansfield on the televised Academy Awards show in 1957; even Dagmar herself on *Broadway Open House* all "accidentally" fell out of their sexy dresses on live TV.[7] It might have sent the censors sputtering and their congressmen fulminating, but after all, it was also good publicity.

The very idea of a Dagmar in their living rooms offended some citizens mightily, and they complained to their congressmen, who duly responded by passing a resolution calling on the House of Representatives to conduct a "full and complete investigation and study to determine the extent to which radio and television programs contain immoral or offensive material."[8] That duty fell to the aforementioned Congressman Gathers, who already had singled out Dagmar for opprobrium, calling her low-cut gowns, ahem, a "little different."[9]

Gathers and his subcommittee terrified the stations and the networks, and rightly so. After all, in those early years of TV, station licenses came up for review and renewal every single year, and Congress, hunting for Hollywood Reds, seemed quite capable of mandating censorship and yanking licenses, too.

Over at CBS, the so-called Tiffany Network, the very word "sex" was promptly banned from being uttered over the airwaves, while at one Chicago TV station a stunt-loving disk jockey was instantly fired after he and a willing starlet tweaked the new code with a five minute on-air "kiss." In response to the Gathers hearings, in wardrobe rooms all around Hollywood, gauze began to be routinely sewn onto low-cut gowns. A "girl" planning to go on television in a sweater deemed too tight had to change her top, and if she dared to display nipples that were visible through the fabric of her top, the offending projections were taped right over.

But even in the upright, uptight, downright scarified early fifties, not every voice was shrill and strident, or feared that too much skin and shenanigans on TV would lead to America's ruination. In Los Angeles, Hal Humphrey, one of the pioneers of daily-newspaper television criticism, thought that more sexiness was just what the new medium needed.

"What's so wrong with putting a little sex and romance into your home?" genial, folksy Humphrey asked, quoting—approvingly—a "tall, shapely" young TV actress named Joan Shawlee, who'd been hired to play a "devastating vamp" on a Bob Hope TV sketch and, accordingly, had been outfitted in a daring dress.

"The neckline was cut down to here and the skirt was slit up the side to there!" Miss Shawlee exclaimed, before confiding to the TV columnist that, at the show's final rehearsal, "one of the sponsor's representatives" had pronounced the costume "too risqué" and a wardrobe woman had been instructed to "sew it up."[10]

Of the "Threat to Morality" posed by "Plunging Necklines on TV," the threat being condemned in the hallowed halls of the United States Congress, Humphrey opined: "Despite all the to-do about the gals and their half-shell bras, they have been easily responsible for selling as many sets to the male side of the population as Gorgeous George and Baron Leone [two TV wrestlers] have sold to the fair sex.

"For the telecasters themselves voluntarily to jettison one of their major attractions at a time when TV set sales are not too brisk anyway seems not only foolhardy but downright dumb."[11]

Besides, Humphrey continued, "There's been no indication from the House Un-American Activities Committee that it has found anything subversive about a gal displaying some of nature's charms on video, nor did Sen. Kefauver include thirty-six-inch busts as a form of the numbers racket."[12]

Senator Estes Kefauver was the Tennessee Democrat who became nationally prominent when the Senate Committee to Investigate Organized Crime in Interstate Commerce, which he chaired, held hearings in 1950 and 1951. Those were the first hearings televised nationally by the fledgling medium of television. Politicians for generations had been attracting the spotlight by crusading against crime and sex, and Kefauver promptly followed up the organized-crime hearings by forming a subcommittee to investigate the ties between pornography and juvenile delinquency. Bettie Page, the cult pinup queen of the early fifties, was probably the most prominent figure to be caught up in the subcommittee's net.

When Page's under-the-counter cheesecake and fetish photos came to light in the Kefauver hearings, her budding TV career, which had already included appearances on *The Jackie Gleason Show* and *The Earl Wilson Show*, was abruptly over and she vanished from public sight.

Humphrey's advice to the broadcasters so eager to accommodate the politicians by censoring themselves was: "The smartest thing to do is spend all their waking hours developing something which might conceivably take the place of semi-nude female chests."[13]

BY 1953, BROADCAST TELEVISION WAS MERELY HALF A DECADE old, yet more than half the homes in the United States already had a television set. Only a year before the Federal Communications Commission (FCC) had lifted its freeze on new television licenses, and tall towers and TV stations were multiplying all across the land. It was early in the Eisenhower Era, but already the music seemed to be getting louder (and faster) and the kids seemed to be getting more unruly. And the same things that were bubbling in the culture at large were beginning to turn up on television, too.

Fittingly enough, perhaps the first, oblique prime-time recognition that there *was* a sexual dimension to real life—just a hint of the shadowy Beast With Two Backs—came in 1953 on *I Love Lucy* (1951–1957), the most popular show in America.

"SINCE WE SAID 'I DO,' THERE ARE SO MANY THINGS WE DON'T."

So said Lucy Ricardo on October 15, 1951, during the premiere episode of the new half-hour comedy on CBS, which, in a few short months, became the first-ever example of a "Must See" TV sitcom in the new medium's history, practically bringing the nation's business to a stop every Monday night.

Lucy and Desi, Fred and Ethel: They were beloved and they were funny and there was a gentle timelessness to their misadventures—crushing grapes in a giant vat, say, or working on a speedy candy assembly line—that continue to air around the world to this day. Nothing in the early 1950s could dent that popularity—not the revelation that Lucille Ball had once belonged to the Communist Party (she'd registered as a young woman only to placate her aging radical grandfather she said, and that was that), and certainly not even the revelation that the most popular figure on American television was having a baby. Although that's exactly what her advertiser (a tobacco company) and some network executives feared.

Regardless of whatever it was that she and Desi had stopped doing since saying "I do," clearly they were still having sex, and Lucy and Desi's decision to incorporate the pregnancy into their hit TV show proved it gloriously, if implicitly.

The sponsor and network suggestions that the pregnancy be hidden, with Lucy standing behind furniture or otherwise dressed up and filmed in such ways as to disguise her in-a-family-way condition was not something they were willing to do.

Nothing needed to be said (nor in the climate of the fifties could it be), but the sight of a *real* pregnant woman playing a pregnant woman on television—for the first time ever—was an eloquent illustration of the unspoken subject. Women around the country, pregnant in record numbers during those first, fecund years of the Baby Boom, did not fail to notice.

The first pregnancy episode was called "Lucy Is Enceinte" ("enceinte" is a French word meaning "with child"), and it was even vetted by three local religious leaders before being filmed. In it the word "pregnant" is never mentioned. Instead, Lucy first tells Ethel she's feeling a bit "dauncey," which, she explains, was her grandmother's word for when you're "not really sick, but you feel lousy." And she adds, she's been putting on a lot of weight. Ethel gets it right away, as did the audience, and the episode ends on an emotional note, with Lucy telling Desi at the Tropicana Club that she is "expecting."

It was the first of seven pregnancy episodes that included "Lucy Hires an English Tutor," so the baby wouldn't grow with Ricky's accent, and "Ricky Has Labor Pains," in which Ricky develops sympathetic morning sickness.

In January 1953, the birth of Desi Arnaz Jr., in both real life and on his parents' TV show on the same day, created a media sensation. Forty-four million people tuned in to watch "Lucy Goes to the Hospital," the birth episode, which represented a stunning 71.7 share of the audience.[14]

In all the hoopla and genuine joy, the word "sex" had never been mentioned, but it was there nonetheless as subtext, and it gave an entirely new resonance to the words "I Love Lucy."

On the *Lucy* show, behavior we now see as sexual was played for innocent laughs. For example, when Lucy behaved "like a child," Ricky was not above putting her across his knee and spanking her. The result, before the inevitable fade to black, was merely a comical "Waaaah!" And if they ever played around in the bedroom with handcuffs, as they did in one 1952 episode, it was because Lucy had locked them together as part of one of her schemes and then couldn't get the cuffs off. So of course Ricky had to go on stage and sing, with Lucy acting as his animated right arm behind the curtain.

Lucy's persistent efforts to break into show business was one long-term theme on the show. Misunderstandings about matrimonial matters was another. In one episode Lucy fears Ricky is "losing interest," and when playing the femme fatale at breakfast gets no results, she tries being a poker-playing pal; in another, she fends off the unwanted attentions of a dirty old man. And in another, Lucy, whose lips are literally sealed, pantomimes a juicy bit of gossip for Ethel, acting out the story of a neighbor who catches her husband out dancing with another woman. In yet another, when Lucy and Ethel declare they want to be "equal," Ricky and Fred respond by getting separate checks after a nice restaurant meal. "Equal rights," says Ricky. And he and Fred leave the wives, who are unable to pay, to do dishes.

The episode that came closest to risqué involved joking about adultery—though of course the word itself was never uttered. Nor did anybody say "affair" or "fooling around" or any of the many synonyms and suggestive circumlocutions so commonplace on primetime today.

When Ricky secretly visits sexy Mrs. Grace Foster, a neighbor lady in a low-cut sun dress, while saying he's going to see Fred, Lucy gets suspicious. And when Ethel tells her she's just seen Ricky coming out of the Foster's apartment, and, moreover, that Mr. Foster is out of town, Lucy breaks down.

"Waaaaah," she wails.

Later, a guy down at the Tropicana Nightclub, where Ricky's rehearsing the band, rushes in to announce that a "dame called. . . . . She says she'll phone you when the coast is clear."

"It's business," insists Ricky, but of course nobody believes him.

Neither does Fred. "Oh yah?" he says dubiously. "Not 'oh yah,'" Ricky protests.

And later when Mrs. Foster calls, Lucy listens in on the extension, devastated to hear Mrs. Foster ask, "Does Lucy suspect anything yet?" and Ricky to reply, "We got her fooled."

"It's all true," she wails to Ethel when Ricky sneaks out to the Foster's apartment again. "I've lost him! . . . He flew to her waiting arms."

But of course, there's an innocent "splanation": Ricky knows that Mr. Foster works at a jewelry store and he wants to buy real pearls for Lucy as an anniversary present. He's glad to get Mrs. Foster's promise of a 20 percent discount, too, because real pearls are "so darned 'spensive."

Before you can say oh no not again, Ethel and Lucy have put on painters' caps and white overalls and lowered themselves down the outside of the building, holding on to ropes at opposite sides of a narrow scaffolding.

While Ricky and Mrs. Foster are inside, and he's innocently helping her unclasp a pearl necklace from around her neck, we see the two "painters" pantomiming hilariously out the window. Lucy, aghast, lets go of her end of the rope. Then the scaffold tilts almost vertically. Lucy and Ethel momentarily disappear, only to rise again, buckets of gloppy paint upended on their heads.

"There's been an accident," Fred yells, running in, and he and Ricky pull the two women inside and the funny misunderstanding—no, Ricky is not having an affair with the sexy neighbor lady—is unraveled in a few final moments.

Lucille Ball, the reigning queen of TV comedy, wasn't simply a funny lady, she was a savvy one, too, filming her shows in color years before color television broadcasts were the norm. When she became pregnant, she and Desi knew the viewers would understand. That's because young married adult Americans were having babies in record numbers. In fact, it was the beginning of the Baby Boom. And the sponsor, reluctant to go along at first, benefited from the first national media sensation of the TV age.

In those days, people gathered around the office water cooler to talk about what they'd seen on TV, and anyone who was young then will remember all the morning-after talk about what was, in effect, the missing term in the episodes dealing with pregnancy and birth: namely, the sex. If Lucy and Ricky were doing it, then the possibilities might be, well, not exactly endless.

IN MOST REFERENCE BOOKS AT THAT TIME THE ENTRY FOR "HOmosexuality" directed the reader to "See Perversion," and crossdressing was played strictly for vaudeville laughs by the likes of Uncle Miltie (Milton Berle, the shtick comic, who was the medium's first Mr. Television).

A rare exception to the prevalent blinkered mainstream morality was a very sober and very late-night discussion show called *Open Mind,* which brought viewers none other than anthropologist Margaret Mead in a "general" discussion of the subject of homosexuality in various cultures.

The program generally passed by without receiving many remarks. Along with the advertisers, the censors seemingly kept early-to-bed, early-to-rise hours, mostly ignoring programming with minuscule audiences (and ad rates) in the wee hours. So while the censors continued to patrol prime time, early glimmers of a more torrid world were turning up in late night, not only on serious discussion shows, but in the person of the local news "weather girl" and the late movie "hostess."

For all the alarms of the guardians of public morality, sex on TV in the early and mid-fifties was mostly a matter of the very sporadic "blue" joke slipped into a comedy routine.

In the aftermath of the great "Plunging Necklines" debate, if you actually wanted to *see* something sexy on television in the mid-1950s, you were best advised to stay up late, watching for that brief but deliciously cheesy moment before your local station aired its Friday or Saturday night horror movie. This was when Vampira, a slinky apparition from a Charles Addams cartoon—or one of her many imitators in the bigger markets around the country—introduced the weekly offering, perhaps *I Walk With a Zombie, Cat People,* or some other old Val Lewton movie, returning with a suggestive, vampy routine between commercials.

The sexy "Mistress of Ceremonies for Old Movies" phenomenon arguably reached its height, in Los Angeles at least, with Voluptua (1955) on the local ABC station.

Voluptua was actually a sexy, young blonde pinup model, tall (5´9˝) and busty (39-24-37), with a pronounced Brooklyn accent. Hers was the classic Tinseltown story. Twenty-five-year-old Gloria Pall, the former Miss Flatbush of 1947, had emigrated to Hollywood in search of fame and fortune, but had found only bit parts. As Voluptua, though, wearing wispy negligees and tight lounging pajamas, she captivated everyone. For all those prepubescent Baby Boomer boys staying up late, the very ones the moral guardians were trying to protect, she was nothing less than "Must Sneak" TV.

"Welcome to my boudoir," she would croon, waving a hand at a stage set equipped with a queen-size circular couch, a statue of Venus de Milo, a white bear rug, and a translucent screen, behind which Voluptua retired to change clothes at least once per performance.

"I want you to feel," she would begin, "that this is your special hideaway.

"Relax. . . . Take off your shoes. . . . Loosen your tie. . . . Clothes are one of my *two* big weaknesses"—nudge, nudge—"as you can see.

"But this [outfit] is a little too formal for our date. So I hope you'll forgive me if I slip out of it. Here, in my suite, when I'm alone with you, I know I can just be myself.

"I always sleep in men's pajama tops. They're so roomy. . . . I'll be with you . . . in my dreams. . . .[15]

And then, as the camera glided in for a tight close-up, she would pucker up and plant a big kiss.

SEXY MATERIAL WAS TURNING UP AS WELL AS ON DAYTIME TV, where the morality plays of the soap operas, often imported directly from radio, held sway.

"Sex is important to us because our audience wants it," Albert McCleery, a daytime producer of the time best known for the suggestively titled 1942 film comedy, *The Lady Is Willing,* pronounced grandiloquently to another TV columnist of the period.[16] "We've got . . . the young housewife in the afternoon, the young married women between twenty-one and twenty-nine. They do most of the purchasing and they're the audience the sponsor is after," he said. "Sex is all a woman thinks about while she's sitting at home, and we can give it to her." Perhaps, but never in prime time. The kids were home then and glued to the set.

A dancer-actress on one variety show, performing a modern dance routine to "One O'Clock Jump," for example, soon found herself accused of doing a "bump and grind,"[17] and she told TV

columnist Hal Humphrey she was considering getting out of
the TV business because of the distressing condemnation.
Nonetheless, Sheree North went on to a successful career in
both TV and films.

Criticizing a tyro TV actress in the mid-fifties was one thing—
that could be done with impunity—but televised bumping and
grinding by the king of rock and roll was another matter entirely.
Or was it?

SEX WAS WHAT THE CENSORS WERE WORRIED ABOUT WHEN ELVIS
Presley appeared on Ed Sullivan's show, the most popular variety
hour of the period. Elvis Presley was a sensation with preteen
girls, who shrieked and cried and pressed, arms outstretched im-
ploringly, toward the stage wherever he sang, and more importantly, whenever he sneered and gyrated his hips and shoulders.

He had appeared on other variety shows of the time, including
those hosted by the Dorsey brothers, Uncle Miltie, and Steve
Allen, where he sang "You Ain't Nothin' But a Hound Dog" to an
actual hound dog. But still, the concerned and the censorious
folks pondered his impending 1956 appearance on the ultra-
popular *Talk of the Town,* Sullivan's show, with horror. What would
letting the barbaric spectacle into the nation's homes do to the
morals of the nation's young?

Ed Sullivan, the "Great Stone Face" of fifties television and one
of TV's earliest and most powerful arbiters of pop culture, ran his
show to a strict moral standard. His producers had no compunc-
tion about demanding costume alterations from female performers to cover up a bosomy chest, including forcing a singer once to
wear her low-cut gown backward.

Sullivan had long refused to book the rock and roll sensation,
who'd been denounced as a "disciple of the devil" for his "lewd"

performances. A man very much of the old school, Ed Sullivan was more comfortable with the vaudeville-like progression of Broadway dancers, show-tune singers, magicians, and acrobats who comprised his typical show. But when Elvis appeared on *The Steve Allen Show,* Ed's new competition, it was Ed who lost the ratings war. And that's when Sullivan saw the light. He capitulated to the King with an unprecedented offer of fifty thousand dollars for three appearances.[18]

Elvis had been a ratings draw on those other variety shows, and in talking to columnists and TV hosts he always came off as a polite and modest lad. Still to many, rock and roll was the devil's music and Presley the devil's imp incarnate. So when Elvis first appeared, Sullivan's producers reacted predictably, careful to pull back or cut away whenever he went into anything more controversial than a sneer and a shrug.

But Sullivan's show, the most popular in America, with the power to ratify a performer's legitimacy and drawing power, gave Presley an almost incredible level of exposure. His first appearance in 1956 drew a smashing 82.6 share of the audience (meaning more than eight out of every ten people in front of a TV set at that hour were tuned in to Elvis); his second appearance beat the nearest competition by a margin of two to one. And on his third and final appearance, standoffish Sullivan gave Elvis the ultimate accolade, calling him a "real decent, fine boy."[19] Worried parents and other concerned Americans may have been somewhat mollified, but his moves still drove the teenage (and even older) girls in the audience wild.

But the Elvis moves had a message, and the new medium of television broadcast that message nationwide: Elvis told teenage girls, as one observer so perceptively had it, that "it was okay to have a body from the waist down—and to move it."[20]

FAMILY VALUES, IN THE FOLKSY PERSONS OF THE NELSONS and the Cleavers—and in all those other nuclear families where Father knew best because he was the breadwinner, and Mom delighted in her full-time job of housekeeper, cook, and folk wisdom-dispensing power behind the scenes—were generally the only values depicted in prime time.

If, for example, the Beav's older brother, Wally, suddenly began acting mysterious and, well, strange—and he was discovered to be keeping company with Eddie Haskell's dimply cute girlfriend in the Angora sweater—why, there was nothing untoward going on...even when the two backlighted shadows in her window appeared to be embracing. Aw shucks, why it's just good-hearted pal Wally being fitted for the sweater Eddie's girlfriend is knitting as a birthday present for her suspicious beau!

And when "jazz detective" Johnny Staccato (John Cassavetes, the patron saint of American independent cinema, who starred in *Staccato,* a short-lived series) is shown getting a rather "passionate" massage from a "beatnik girl," how does he react? Why, he ignores her of course!

And what does Johnny Yuma (Nick Adams), TV's Western *Rebel,* do when a pretty girl offers him *more than money,* if only he'll save her condemned father's life? Yup, pard'ner, he ignores her—jes' the way Marshal Dillon treats Miss Kitty on *Gunsmoke.*

"Sex manifests itself in strange ways on TV," observed sage columnist Hal Humphrey, considering these and similarly dramatic situations.[21] Yes, indeed.

One of the strangest, and arguably most far-reaching, manifestations was the wildly successful Clairol hair-coloring advertising campaign that began in 1956. Innocent on the glossy surface and absolutely of their time in every other way, the TV commercials about the pert and perfectly coiffed blondes all shared a most provocative tag line that included the most famous double entendre in American advertising history . . . . *Does she or doesn't she?*

Meanwhile, elsewhere . . .

As the fifties gave way to the sixties . . .

In Japan, *The Pink Mood Show,* only fifteen minutes long and broadcast once a week on Sunday nights, captured a remarkable 54 percent of the national viewing audience. Why?

It was unabashed burlesque on the home screen: *Girls Girls Girls*—bumping, grinding, dancing, and strip teasing— in bikinis, nightgowns, and *LESS!*

BY THE END OF THE 1950S, WITH THAT HUGE BABY BOOMER generation entering the rebellious teenage years and Senator John Fitzgerald Kennedy heralding a new era and entering the race for the White House, TV executives began importing the high-minded discussion of formerly taboo subjects, à la *Open Mind,* to day time, too.

Joyce Brothers, a young psychologist, first became a household name when she appeared on TV as a contestant on *The $64,000 Question.* Improbably, boxing was her area of expertise. She parlayed that media spotlight into a short-lived but influential daily talk show. On it, she dispensed matter-of-fact advice on such formerly forbidden subjects as menopause and frigidity. It was one of the original templates for a trend that would evolve into racy daytime talk shows within a decade, morphing, after a full quarter century, into trash and tabloid TV.

Before the fifties faded into history, a full 88 percent of U.S. homes had at least one television set. But the shocking TV morality issue that most vexed the public then didn't have a thing to do with TV sex.

The decade that began with one congressional committee looking into the sexual morality of television ended with another committee delving into the moral and ethical questions raised by the high-stakes TV quiz shows that had so mesmerized the country, shows just like the one that brought Dr. Brothers her original fame...and which turned out to have been fixed.

The Sixties

The Great Wasteland, from Hooterville to Peyton Place

"A VAST WASTELAND," NEWTON MINOW, THE LIBERAL-LEANING chairman of the Federal Communications Commission called the medium he was charged with regulating in 1961, when sex on television was still just a shimmering mirage. (A quarter century later, he wittily amended that remark to "half-vast.")

The first birth control pills became available at the beginning of the decade, but TV morality was still generally a clear-cut, black and white issue, and programming was still governed by the Code of Ethics. TV's dominant prime time programming genre was the so-called "adult" Western, shows from *Gunsmoke* to *Bonanza,* and it was governed by its own code, that of the West, which meant that Marshal Dillon always plugged the bad guy, but hardly ever seemed to find time for the ever-willing Miss Kitty.

But even then, at the very edge of the stark wasteland were some signs of the colorfulness to come. In 1962, on NBC late night, Jack Paar, the tightly-wrapped host of *The Tonight Show,* stalked off the air after a censor vetoed a joke that referred to the "w.c."—which stood for "water closet," that is, the bathroom toilet—and was promptly replaced by a young, easy-going former quiz show host named Johnny Carson, whose engaging manner allowed him to fire off double-entendres and risqué observations that would have been impossible before.

Meanwhile, elsewhere...

On New Year's Eve, 1963, while American's were clinking glasses to the soothing televised strains of Guy Lombardo, Parisians were mesmerized by Brigitte Bardot's half-hour, one-woman special. The sexpot blonde star of *And God Created Woman* sang, danced, and played guitar, and for the big musical finale—ooh la la!—wore only clingy, flesh-colored tights, covered strategically by vine leaves.

BACK ON PRIME TIME, EVEN THOUGH A HAPPILY MARRIED COUPLE might for the first time be shown together in a single bed, generally the rule of censor's thumb was that the "wife," even if covered by a blanket, must be understood to be wearing a nightgown. That led to one network's explicit "strap" requirement: that is, to avoid the implication of under-the-sheets nudity, the viewer should be able to see at least a single shoulder strap on the wife's nightgown peeking over the top of the blanket in any married couple's bedroom scene.

In 1963, about the same time the first Boomer kids were reaching college, CBS, the perpetual ratings leader in the first era of

American television, had no fewer than fourteen of the top fifteen series on the air. Many appealed to an older, more rural mass audience that was supposed to like shows such as *Petticoat Junction,* set in the small town of Hooterville, a place where nothing much of consequence ever happened and where smiley, bouncy, big-eyed Billie Jo, Betty Joe, and Bobby Jo apparently bathed regularly in the town's water supply.

(CBS's appeal to older viewers continues to this very day. At the end of 1999, for example, the median age of CBS viewers was 53.1 years old. By contrast, the median age of viewers of the WB, the youngest of the six broadcast networks, was 28.7.[22] The median age of the U.S. population is around 35.)

The very next season, ABC, the newest, scrappiest network, counter-attacked by counter-programming CBS's older- and more rural-skewing programs with what was the original demographic-oriented schedule. Debuting the very same September week were not only *Voyage to the Bottom of the Sea, The Addams Family,* and *Bewitched,* but *Shindig*—a half hour of dancers in calf-high boots and short shorts go-go dancing to the kind of pop music satirized in *Austin Powers*—and *Peyton Place,* a *nighttime* soap, starring a young and ethereal Mia Farrow as the young and ethereal Allison McKenzie. In the debut episode, Allison predicted wanly that the town's richest boy, whom she'd just spurned, would tell "everybody that I'm frigid."

It was a risky schedule, and no risk was greater than importing the risqué ethos of a daytime soap to prime time. Would audiences be affronted by the joyless bed hopping of the mostly married adults in the picturesque New England town of Peyton Place, which was far from down-home Hooterville? Would they rebel, tuning out and sending skittish advertisers fleeing for the entrenched competition?

Touch that dial? Not on your life! In its first season the show—boosted perhaps by the very public real-life affair between young Mia and singer Frank Sinatra, then at the height of his swinging Rat Pack prowess—became so successful that original half-hour episodes were broadcast *three times a week.*

When Mia left the production to go on a romantic cruise with her paramour, the writers fell back on that old soap opera standby, the coma. And the producers found a look-alike stand-in for the brief shots of comatose "Allison" in bed.

Sexy talk about adultery on a prime-time soap was one thing. Sober drama about teenage venereal disease was another—despite all those rock-crazed Boomer teens cruising around in their jalopies, and despite the indisputable fact that, quite clearly, VD had reached epidemic proportions by the mid-sixties.

Thanks partly to TV, the new generation of teenagers was, as one critic put it, obsessed with "dancing and sex." So it was no surprise that in 1964, a year in which, according to the U.S. Surgeon General, "Fifteen hundred young Americans [become] new victims of venereal diseases every day," two NBC series from MGM—*Mr. Novak,* about a high school teacher, and *Dr. Kildare,* a popular doctor show—came up with a shared two-part plot about a seventeen-year-old boy who contracts syphilis. It was, quite simply, the socially responsible thing to do.

The boy in the story confides to the good Doctor Kildare (Richard Chamberlain) that he's "been with" three girls, and at first he's distraught and suicidal. Eventually, the boy learns an important lesson about syphilis—that it's highly communicable, but treatable. Happy ending, lesson learned.

The story would begin in *Novak's* high school and end in *Kildare's* hospital, but the writers and producers hadn't counted on network censors, who, despite direct pleas by the Surgeon General of the United States and the American Medical Association, declared any discussion of sexual intercourse or intimation of teen sex "inappropriate for family viewing." The joint episodes never aired.

One season before, however, *The Nurses,* a CBS medical drama, aired a venereal disease episode without controversy or protest. A couple of seasons later, the National Association of Broadcasters withdrew its seal of approval from several stations that had the temerity to air...a hemorrhoid cure commercial.

Meanwhile, the censors themselves were more apt to be pondering the permissible prime-time level of bouncy exuberance for starlet Jill St. John, shown running around in a bikini when NBC debuted *Fame Is the Name of the Game* in 1966. The censors demanded that the offending scene be cut, and that demand was duly reported by the press.

Because *Fame* was an important factor in the development of the network's two-hour TV movie "franchise" under the "World Premiere" marquee, the scene may have been filmed, and publicized, precisely to draw attention to the telefilm. It was, in any event, not cut outright, but merely "trimmed," demonstrating yet again that censorship in the sixties could be affected by economic considerations and was, above all, capricious.

At the same time, a significant TV breakthrough was passing without much notice, either at the time or later. It was presented in such a wholesome and all-American manner that only the most reactionary and bigoted could call it controversial.

That breakthrough was central to *I Spy* (1965–1968), a one-hour spy drama, set (and filmed) in various exotic locales around the world. It was comedian Bill Cosby's first series.

Sure, two decades later *The Cosby Show* was funny and pro-social and proved that a fifties sitcom could work in the eighties, too (and it almost single-handedly reversed the fortunes of its lagging network, NBC), but the really significant expansion of TV viewers' horizons came earlier, when Cosby was paired with Robert Culp. They were Alexander Scott and Kelly Robinson, respectively, two globe-trotting playboy tennis pros, glib and hip and bright, secretly working for the CIA.

The show also was significant in the history of the medium's technology. The light-weight, mobile TV studio that could be packed up and stowed in an airplane, which was developed for *I Spy* by Fouad Said, enabled the production to go out for extended shoots in the most distant locations, from Hong Kong to Spain to Mexico, filming out in the streets and countryside in a way still unsurpassed by present-day dramas. But more importantly, this was the first series to portray an unmarried black man in a realistic way, on equal terms socially with his white partner, and that most definitely included sexy girlfriends and his own love life.

Meanwhile, elsewhere...

On the other side of the Atlantic...

While Americans were transfixed by the scandalous goings-on in *Peyton Place* on ABC, in England the staid British Broadcasting Corporation aired a sketch titled "Naked as Nature Expected" on BBC-3, a brand-new satirical show.

The 1965 sketch poked fun at the so-called "nudist pictures," which were low-budget movies that, under the guise of

continued on next page

continued from previous page

anthropological, fun-in-the-sun theatrical documentaries, specialized in presenting nature-loving, volleyball-playing young
ladies, tanned all over, frolicking in the buff.

Accordingly, the BBC sketch depicted a nudist wedding,
showing a bride naked except for her strategically held bou-
quet, a groom naked except for his traditional top hat, and their
completely nude bridesmaids in the background. It aired, according to a news report of the time, without a single word of
viewer protest.

Interestingly enough, at almost the same time, on a late-
night BBC panel show, playwright and critic Kenneth Tynan,
then the literary director of Britain's National Theater, provoked
a howl of public outrage when he uttered the word "fuck" in a
discussion of the limits of sexuality in the legitimate theater.

And a few months later, the once staid BBC, known to the
British viewing public as Auntie Beeb, was at it again, this time
broadcasting a special in which a twentysomething couple was
shown in bed.

The young woman was topless. Both she and the young man
were aspiring actors who'd been encouraged to improvise, and
so earnestly discussed such subjects as incest, lesbianism and
their respective losses of virginity.

KINKY, BABY! LONG BEFORE *AUSTIN POWERS* SPOOFED SIXTIES
secret-agent superheroes, Diana Rigg and Patrick Macnee, as Mrs.
Emma Peel and Mr. John Steed, were doing it on the British import *The Avengers* (1966–1969).

In fact, almost all the shows on American television in the mid-
to late sixties and early 1970s with the highest sexual content, from

The Avengers to the 1971 *Elizabeth R* miniseries, which aired on PBS and included a brief glimpse of full-frontal female nudity, to *All in the Family,* which was based on a 1966 British series titled *'Till Death Do Us Part,* seemed to originate from the mother country.

The Avengers' Mrs. Peel was a sometimes leather-clad young widow (and therefore sexually experienced), who'd mastered martial arts and could shoot the cork out of a champagne bottle, which was fortunate indeed, because Mr. Steed was a Pierre Cardin-attired, bowler-topped dandy armed only with a bumbershoot. They shared, however, a taste for impeccable stylishness and fine bubbly.

Diana Rigg was the most memorable of several partners for the dapper Mr. Steed. (In *The New Avengers,* the short-lived, mid-seventies reprise, Steed's foil was "Purdey," played by the same Joanna Lumley who went on to incarnate Patsy Stone so deliciously in *Absolutely Fabulous.*) Fittingly enough, Rigg, an auburn-haired English rose with flawless skin and a detached and ironic manner, joined the show when Macnee's previous partner, the honey-blonde actress Honor Blackman, left to join Sean Connery in *Goldfinger,* in which she played the part of the lesbian aviatrix Pussy Galore.

The Avengers specialized in outrageous villains and arch dialogue and double entendres that were more than a little shocking on American television in the 1960s. The show even had its own pussy galore episode. In "The Hidden Tiger," which like all *Avengers* episodes was subtitled ("Steed Hunts a Big Cat, Emma is Badly Scratched"), the villains are intent on conquering Britain by turning its entire feline population into crazed, mauling killers. The bad guys go by names like Angora, Dr. Manx, and Edwin Cheshire, who looks like a pudgy cat and, in fact, likes to groom himself and lap at his milk.

The dastardly plot aims to "release the savage beast within," says Mrs. Peel with an ironic smile. "Tear down the barriers of inhibition, run riot." When Steed goes undercover to the villains' headquarters at P.U.R.R. (the Philanthropic Union for the Rescue, Relief, and Recuperation of Cats), ostensibly in search of his missing cat, the hair ball-brained Cheshire naturally inquires after the name of his "beloved pussy."

"Emma," answers Steed drolly.

Emma's coloring?

"Reddish-brown," says Steed.

"What a joy for you it must be," rhapsodizes mad Cheshire, "when she's curled up on your lap."

Indeed. Later, Mrs. Peel repeats the ploy, showing up to find *her* missing cat. And it's name would be . . . .

"Little John," says she. "Very bad tempered first thing in the morning until he's had his first glass of champagne."

Certainly the sexuality was immensely good-humored and played for knowing smirks, if not laughs, but it was definitely a departure and definitely offbeat. Given the times, the show's fondness for leather was, well, kinky, baby.

Consider the sexiest episode of all. "A Touch of Brimstone," in which "Steed Joins the Hellfire Club, and Emma Becomes the Queen of Sin," was considered so racy in its time that it was severely edited before showing in Britain, and it never aired at all in the United States. (It's only recently been released on video by the Arts & Entertainment cable network.) This one has Mrs. Peel undercover again, only this time she's gotten up in a whalebone corset, knee-high lace-up leather boots, and a spiked dog collar (a costume the estimable Ms. Rigg designed herself). Then, in the scene that was edited even in Britain. . . . She's whipped by the dastardly villain!—He's the leader of a modern-day Hellfire Club, modeled after the true original of the same name, an orgiastic brotherhood for the debauched eighteenth-century British elite.

SEX SOLD SOAP, AS THE OLD ADVERTISING TRUISM WENT, AND nowhere more so than in lucrative daytime, where the regular mid-sixties fare included "death, disease, violence, alcoholism, attempted suicide, amnesia, rape, malpractice and child-custody suits"[23]—in other words, a formula that had served soap operas well since radio days. But if the jeopardy and the plots were old, what was new was the increasingly frank talk. On one soap, for example, a girl hid her abortion from her parents with a cover story about ruptured ovarian cysts.[24]

By this time, change also was roiling the larger American society: war in Southeast Asia; sex, drugs and rock and roll at home; and an emerging chasm known as the Generation Gap, across which angry or worried parents yelled at their heedless kids. And though you would've been hard pressed to find a whiff of the New Permissiveness in series prime time, such theatrical features as *Cat on a Hot Tin Roof, What a Way to Go, Never on Sunday* and *The Apartment,* though heavily censored, brought "illicit trystings, adultery, suppressed homosexuality and other overheated carnalities"[25] into the home, as an editorial in one culturally conservative publication harrumphed.

Invariably, the "edited for television," but still sexy, big-screen pictures drew high ratings. So it was inevitable, too, that "The Pursuit of Pleasure" also would become a news event that could then be packaged as an NBC documentary of the same name. *The Pursuit of Pleasure* not only showed pot-smoking hippies turning on, tuning in, and dropping out, but contained a brief snippet of two male bikers kissing as well.

Times they may have been a-changing, and something called

the Sexual Revolution may have been raising the temperature in society at large, but the instincts of the sponsors remained the same. The one-hour *Pleasure* documentary aired as scheduled, but not before its original sponsor, an insurance company, tuned in ahead of time and promptly dropped out too.

Other advertisers were getting the message, however. Where once wholesomeness and inoffensiveness were the order of the day, the newest trend in trendy sixties TV commercials was the sexy sell—blondes having more fun, other blondes breathily urging men shaving in the bathroom to "take it off, take it all off"— and that was working just fine, too.

DESPITE MCCARTHYISM, THE COLD WAR, THE THREAT OF NU-clear conflagration, the "police action" in Korea and other such traumatic events, the decade of the 1950s—as it's been burnished by history—is remembered as a time of unparalleled national calm and peace. Then came the decade of the 1960s: war abroad and at home and shock after shock—from the Kennedy and King assassinations and riots (or uprisings, if you will) in the cities to the Civil Rights Movement and the fight for equality of women and gays.

But no more than a glimmer of the controversies in the streets, right there on the nightly news, was reaching network primetime in the 1960s. With the hegemony of the Three Networks intact, there was no incentive to change the fictional formulae of series TV. In other words, when there was something approaching a national cultural consensus in the 1950s, that consensus was reflected (in an idealized way of course) in series like *Father Knows Best, Leave It to Beaver,* and *The Donna Reed Show* on prime time TV. A decade later, that consensus was shattered in a drumbeat of trau-matic public events:

- The 1962 Cuban Missile Crisis, when for a few days the nation's kids thought they were about to die without ever experiencing the sweaty delights of sex.

- The 1963 assassination of President John Fitzgerald Kennedy, when the new, young president the nation's kids thought would change the world was murdered.

- And then Vietnam, when a faraway jungle war grinding on through the decade actually did kill tens of thousands of the nation's kids.

But very few of those traumas made it to prime time network series, whether dramas or comedies, where the great mass audience captured by the Three Networks continued to be *Bewitched* and to *Dream of Jeannie.*

FUNDAMENTALISTS, TRADITIONALISTS, POLITICALLY CONSERVATIVE social critics, parents who were just plain worried, and all the others concerned about the fraying fabric of society, had been decrying sex on TV since the very birth of the medium—and warning about the slippery-slope dangers of relaxed moral vigilance when it came to the home box. The first TV censorship battles in the fifties were about those "plunging" necklines; a decade and a half later, in the interest of upholding virtue, the censors set their sights even lower. The result was just plain silly.

In the second half of the 1960s, NBC broadcast *I Dream of Jeannie,* a sweet-natured half-hour comedy about the misadventures of a pert, bright-eyed, and two-thousand-year-old genie (Barbara Eden) and her "master," a perpetually confounded astronaut (Larry Hagman), whom Jeannie not-so-secretly loves.

For the role, Ms. Eden was dressed in the "traditional" Hollywood genie costume—headdress, scarf, harem pants, a short Bolero jacket-style top—with a bare midriff, and needless to say she looked adorable. So far, so good. But then came the line in the sand: NO NAVEL! *Never*. Lest community standards be offended, the harem pants must remain waist-high. So decreed the network's censor and so agreed the show's creator, who, not so incidentally, was Sidney Sheldon—the same Sidney Sheldon who would go on to become a best-selling writer of books whose popularity depended to no small extent on their racy subject matter.

It didn't seem to matter either that *Rowan & Martin's Laugh-In*, an influential and fast-paced sketch comedy show that came along in 1968 and aired on the same network, in fact right after *Jeannie*, showed bikini-clad dancers (among them, an unknown Goldie Hawn) who most definitely did bare their navels, or that Mary Ann got to show hers on *Gilligan's Island*.

"They tell me it had something to do with the Television Code," "Jeannie" herself told an interviewer. "I don't know why. *Laugh-In* has shown navels. They paint flowers around them. Does that make any difference?"[26]

Apparently, yes. A plan to have Eden appear on *Laugh-In* and unveil her navel *there* fell through when the chief NBC censor, supported by Sheldon, decreed it to be in "bad taste," explaining, "We have to be careful. Our premise is a half-naked girl and a young man...she's after."[27] It would be another decade and a half, in the inevitable mid-eighties reunion movie, before the waiting world was afforded its first glimpse of Jeannie's belly button.

Today, most of these early issues and the affronted complaints, about "blue" jokes and décolletage and exposed navels, strike most of us as hopelessly old-fashioned and perhaps quaint. But as the Boomers reached adulthood in the beginning of the 1970s, something new—and genuinely shocking—was flickering to life at home. The whole disco-going country was about to get wired, and it was going to be a wild ride.

The Seventies

All in the Family, M*A*S*H, and *The Ugly George Hour of Truth, Sex, and Violence*

BY THE TIME THE BIGGEST CITIES WERE FINALLY BEING WIRED for cable television in the late 1960s and early 1970s, after years of opposition from traditional over-the-air broadcasters, the heated debate between "free" and "pay" TV had been vexing the TV industry for years.

Cable had started out modestly enough, as a way to extend television to those beyond the reach of programming sent out from tall towers over the "airwaves," signals that could be blocked by mountains or even skyscrapers. But cable's potential to siphon off audiences from the Three Networks' mass audience was always clear enough.

What will you do, the critics of cable (usually the owners of networks or TV stations) huffed, when the World Series becomes pay-per-view?

But as it happened, cable's growth wasn't fueled by high-visibility,

big-ticket sporting events—those came later—so much as it was by
the lure of the formerly forbidden: "art" pictures with plenty of
skin; X-rated "porn" films, movies like *I Am Curious (Yellow)* and
Naked and Free (uncut and in your home!); and the lowest of no-
budget homemade sex videos on the public-access channels.

"Public access," the channels set aside originally by each big-
city cable system, had been designed to give individual citizens a
voice on television, demonstrating cable's outstanding public-
service potential. It was, for example, mandated in Manhattan in
1972 by the local franchising authority. It quickly evolved there
and elsewhere, however, into a come one, come all censorship-
free zone for shows such as *Midnight Blue* and, later, *The Ugly
George Hour of Truth, Sex, and Violence.*

The proto-Howard Stern host of *Ugly George* had his own
boxy, shoulder-held Sony video camera and specialized in filming
himself chatting up girls passing by on the New York streets, then
crudely propositioning them to come up to his squalid apartment
and have videotaped sex.

Did they? Would they?

For certain agog Manhattanites it became must-watch.

A few years before, the phenomenal success of the original sex-
talk radio call-in shows, such as *Feminine Forum* in Los Angeles,
had demonstrated the public's appetite for ordinary folks talking
about doing outrageous, sexy things. Then, seemingly overnight
in the early seventies, unpolished if not exactly "average" people
were gleefully using the public-access channels in Manhattan and
elsewhere not just to *talk* about it, but to do it—to smear food on
their naked bodies, to show off the results of their sex-change op-
erations, and to dance naked for any home viewer with a cable
converter box to see.

Where once the very word "penis" was anathema, now anyone

who could afford cable could see penises and vaginas and all manner of X-rated hardcore action without ever having to leave the privacy of home.

IN WASHINGTON, D.C., RICHARD MILHOUS NIXON WAS PRESIdent, and from the beginning he viewed himself as beleaguered, fighting wars on two fronts: in Southeast Asia, a real conflict, bloody and protracted; at home, a cultural war for the hearts and minds of the badly divided citizenry.

President Nixon was leader not merely of the Free World, but also of something he called the Silent Majority. His allies were prepared to challenge the licenses of broadcasters who opposed him politically, or culturally, defying the Silent Majority's "traditional," "moral" values by broadcasting "sleaze."

"The ultimate irony," said the new Republican chairman of the Federal Communications Commission of the shocking new phenomenon of X-rated public-access programs, "is that the boundaries of the First Amendment may next be tested in the context of the right to broadcast garbage." And it was in this overheated and yeasty climate that *All in the Family* premiered on CBS in 1971.

Even while imparting pro-social values and humanistic advice, the Stivics and the Bunkers were quite capable of droll ribaldry—and some heat, too.

Consider the episode in which Michael Stivic, also known as Meathead (Rob Reiner), finds himself suddenly impotent and his wife Gloria (Sally Struthers) goes to her mother for advice.

"It's probably somethin' that's just goin' around," suggests pixilated Edith (Jean Stapleton), too embarrassed even to say the word "sex."

And later in the episode, when Edith tells Archie (Carroll

O'Connor), ever so obliquely, that Michael has the same unmentionable problem Archie's pal had when he came back from the Army, Archie replies, "Shoosh," grimacing with distaste and waving the entire problem away.

Of course, Gloria takes direct action to inform herself about the "issue" of impotence, calling Doctor Kermit, who advises her that the "problem is often caused by anxiety," such as that experienced by overtired, overworked students studying for finals, which just happens to be a good description of Meathead, her overworked, overstressed husband. When the cause of the anxiety goes away, the problem will too, Gloria concludes sensibly.

The very next night, once Michael has passed all his tests, Gloria puts on a pretty, but not too-sexy dress. The last thing she wants to do, she says, is put pressure on him.

Over at the local saloon, meanwhile, Archie has enlisted George Jefferson, the first black man to move into his working class white neighborhood, for help with what he calls a friend's "connubibal" difficulties.

"He's stuck in neutral."

He's asking, Archie explains deadpan, because "you people" have a "special kind" of stamina.

It's a racial secret all right, Jefferson agrees with mock solemnity, suggesting, "Hog jowls." Twice a day. But watch out for the side effects, he adds—namely, a desire to shine shoes, carry bags, and tap dance.

To howls on the laugh track, Archie ponders this arcane advice, while back in the Bunker living room Michael is still hyperanxious, this time, clearly, because he's worried about whether he'll be able to perform. Plopping down into Archie's favorite chair he tells Gloria nervously that he'd really rather watch a Japanese monster movie than fool around.

Gloria comes over, stands behind him, begins massaging his neck. She massages one shoulder, then begins gently massaging down one arm. All the while Michael continues to watch his movie. When she reaches his hand, she stops and kneels beside his chair.

Finally, he turns to face her, turning away from that hypnotic television at last, and puts his hand on hers.

They look into each other's eyes for a beat. Then, standing together, they both begin to smile, then break into wide, shining-eyed grins. As they kiss, the viewers see only a fade to black, leaving the imagined sex act to come smoldering in any but the simplest viewer's mind, and proving it's not necessarily the most explicit television moment that's the sexiest.

In another *All in The Family* episode, from 1972, innocent Edith answers an ad in a swinger's magazine that's caught her attention because of the "fifty recipes for swingers." The ad, she explains daftly, said a "warm, affectionate, fun-loving couple" wants to "swap good times."

Knock-knock. On cue the wife swappers appear at the Bunkers' door. They turn out to be Ruth and Curtis Rempley (Rue McClanahan and Vincent Gardenia), a couple very much like Edith and Archie, and they've brought presents of fine cigars and expensive perfume.

Later, when Mrs. Jefferson (Isabel Sanford) shows up unexpectedly, she sizes up the situation instantly and warns Edith, who's so innocent she doesn't even know what "wife swappers" are. Meanwhile, Curtis is proudly showing Archie "stag pictures"—of himself and his wife—on a slide viewer.

"There are two dirty people hee-yah," whines Archie, in his most querulous outer-borough drawl.

To the contrary, Ruthie protests primly, "you're looking at a happily married couple."

"A Communist pre-vert," Archie growls.

"Not at all," replies Curtis, drawing himself up like a bantam-rooster; in fact, he points out, he's a Republican.

Swinging saved their marriage, Ruthie adds plaintively. But Ruth and Curtis's conviviality seems forced and desperate, especially after their protestations are met by Edith and Archie's stone-faced disbelief and glaring disapproval. The "happy" swinging couple leaves downcast and dejected.

It wasn't all just catch phrases and shtick, like "Dummy up, Meathead!" and "Stifle yourself, Edith, you dingbat!" or poking fun at intolerance and bigotry, or even using humor on *All in the Family* to send what social scientists are pleased to call a "pro-social" message.

Sometimes the very message itself was edgy, too. Consider the episode in which Gloria returns home distraught, refuses to kiss her husband and, in a voice verging on hysteria, reveals that she's just narrowly escaped being raped. Pulled by a stranger behind the fence of a construction site, a scarf jammed into her mouth, her assailant tearing at her clothes, she was saved—Gloria says between anxious gasps—only because she fainted, and the would-be rapist, thinking she'd died, ran away.

Archie immediately calls in the cops. The detective (Charles Durning) who shows up wearily explains that fewer than 10 percent of the forty thousand rapes committed every year result in convictions in court, often because defense attorneys attack the credibility of the victim and get the attacker off. To show them what he means, the cop asks Gloria a few insinuating questions and finds out she'd not only been wearing a miniskirt, but that she'd once posed nude for a painter friend of her husband's.

"That's all a smart lawyer needs to hear," he says.

Edith, in her inimitable fashion, takes Gloria into the kitchen for a motherly talk. "All day today I been smellin' Rockaway Beach," she says, then tells her daughter about the time she went there as a young woman on a double date and was grabbed and pawed at under the boardwalk. But she too escaped. And she never spoke about it—only to forever wonder how many other women that same man had attacked. "In my time we was too scared to talk open," she says, her face cast down in a worried look.

Gloria returns to the men, at first adamant to testify, but Meathead and Archie have reached a rare agreement that she will *not*. The cop's aggressive demonstration of "smearing" tactics have left her shaken and she doesn't protest when he leaves. "We took care of our own," says Archie as the camera closes in on an extreme close-up of Gloria's face—trembling and inconsolable. Finally, American broadcast-network prime time television had begun to grow up.

Meanwhile, elsewhere...

"Sex and Violence!" "Full Front Nudity!"

Those were also the names of two early episodes of a TV show so irreverent and so controversial that its makers' subsequent professional history included court cases and street protests alike. And what other show with the working title of *Gwen Dibley's Flying Circus* can say that?

By the time the sketch comedy premiered on the BBC in 1969, however, the show's name had become *Monty Python's Flying Circus;* and by the time it began airing in the U.S., its

continued on next page

continued from previous page

troupe of performers—John Cleese, Eric Idle, Terry Gilliam, Graham Chapman, Terry Jones, and Michael Palin—were widely regarded as the Beatles of comedy.

Any listing of *Monty Python's* most memorable salacious moments would be long indeed, but surely would include the "Upper Class Twits," the "Spanish Inquisition," and the unfortunate Arthur Pewty, the bespectacled Milquetoast who's come to realize "only as comparatively recently as recently" that his pneumatic wife Dierdre, even then slipping behind a curtain with the lubricious marriage counselor they're consulting, just might, but only possibly, be somewhat slightly less than, well, totally faithful. And then there were the Royal Canadian Mounties, memorably chorusing

> He's a lumberjack and he's OK,
> He sleeps all night and he works all day.
> He cuts down trees, he skips and jumps,
> He likes to press wild flowers.
> He puts on women's clothing
> And hangs around in bars...?

One of the most influential and arguably the very funniest British TV comedy ever, it was influenced stylistically by America's *Laugh-In*. In turn, its cutout partial animation, accompanied by a plentitude of rude noises and gestures, and such macabre conceits as the baby carriage that devoured its admirers, as well as those quick snippets of bare breasts and the other naughty bits, prefigured *South Park*.

A YEAR BEFORE *ALL IN THE FAMILY*, *THE MARY TYLER MOORE Show* had debuted, and Mare and Ted, and Murr and irascible Mr. Grant continued to mine laughs year after year from the minutiae of work (in a TV newsroom) and dating; and when they tackled a big issue like death, it was the (admittedly hilarious) death of Chuckles the Clown. If topicality intruded, it was invariably with a remark like that of Mary's neighbor, Phyllis, who told a cop in one episode that she was "aware" that the police were objects of controversy, but she was keeping an "open mind."

That Mary Richards had a sex life was suggested, but of course it all occurred far off camera. For example, in one episode in which her parents were visiting, Mary's mother cautions her father not to "forget to take your pill." Without thinking Mary instantly replies: "I won't."

The show was popular partly because it was so well executed and partly because Mary herself was so lovable. But programmers and Madison Avenue advertising executives alike could see that all those Boomer kids finally were growing up and taking control of the TV dial.

And in the polarized climate of the seventies (the Nixon, Ford, and Carter years), the Boomers as a "cohort" clearly stood for more social criticism, more frank talk, more irreverence and, yes please, more sex. And even then it was obvious what the free to be explicit "garbage" on the new and rapidly growing cable competition portended for network ratings.

As the world turned, so did network TV. In daytime, the most profitable "daypart" on television (contributing in some cases a full fifty percent of a network's total profits), the soaps, which for decades had specialized in charting the lives of unhappy families and "straying" husbands and wives, now wove all manner of trendiness and "relevance" into their Byzantine plot lines: abortion, addiction, incest, and impotence became commonplace. One soap story line even "went" to Vietnam, while another actually shot one story arc at a real drug rehab center in New York City, employing real recovering drug addicts as extras in some scenes. Another soap's complex narrative revolved around the "secret" artificial insemination of the family maid.

In 1979, a study found six and one-half "acts of sexual behavior" per single hour of daytime soap—such sociably scientific-sounding activities as "heavy necking," "erotic touching," "verbal" and "visual" intercourse, as well as the incidents of prostitution and rape.

That year, on ABC's *General Hospital,* a character named Luke raped a character named Laura; by 1981, Luke and Laura (Tony Geary and Genie Francis) were the sweethearts of daytime television and their wedding was the highest-rated show on any daytime soap ever.

When she shot the original *G.H.* rape scene, actress Genie Francis was a minor, under eighteen, and NBC censors declared that she couldn't be shown "in bed" with a member of the opposite sex. This meant, according to the twisted logic of censorship avoidance, that the notorious scene had to be staged so that only one actor was "in" bed at any one time, while the other, only half in, kept one foot on the floor.

(Like the TV Code itself, the "one foot on the floor" prohibition was derived partly from the censorship practices and principles first established in the Hays Code, which governed theatrical motion pictures from 1930 until 1968. The Hays Code, formulated to forestall governmental action in the wake of Hollywood sex scandals of the 1920s, contained such strictures as "Excessive and lustful kissing, lustful embraces, suggestive postures and gestures are not to be shown.")

Tony Geary also had played a rapist on CBS's The *Young and the*

Restless, another popular daytime soap. Rapists who later transformed themselves into heroes comprised one of the more despicable narrative mini-trends on the soaps. As far back as the mid-1960s, on *Days of Our Lives,* Bill Horton (Edward Mallory) raped his brother's wife, Laura (Susan Flannery); for years afterward, Laura and Bill conspired to keep Mickey (John Clarke), her husband, from learning that the father of "their" son was really Bill. Even in primetime in the 1980s, a rapist on *Dynasty* one season could become his victim's suitor the next.

ALL THIS WAS RIPE FOR BOTH CANONIZATION AND SATIRE, AND IN the seventies *Mary Hartman, Mary Hartman,* from Norman Lear, played the soap conventions for laughs, while Public Broadcasting's *Upstairs, Downstairs* gave viewers all the furtive couplings, dread family secrets, and outrageous twists of fate, but dressed up with Edwardian costuming and British accents.

Meanwhile, within a few years of coming out on the streets, homosexual characters, though years away from becoming series regulars, were turning up on individual episodes of prime-time series. Lovable, malaprop-spouting bigot Archie Bunker, who weekly blustered against "pinkos," "jungle bunnies," and "gooks" on *All in the Family,* discovered that one of his tough, ex-jock bar buddies was "one a those"—gay. *The Bold Ones,* NBC's doctor/lawyer anthology series, aired an episode in which a girl left her boyfriend for a lesbian lover. Even ABC's *Marcus Welby, M.D.,* the very model of the fatherly medico (played by Robert Young, formerly the paterfamilias of *Father Knows Best*) did a 1973 episode called "The Other Martin Loring," about a married family man who suffered psychosomatic symptoms because of a "confused" sexual identity. The show was picketed because of the episode—not by outraged fundamentalists, however, but by gay activists offended because homosexuality was being depicted as a disease and the good Doctor Welby had prescribed suppression of the unacceptable desire.

With the exception of *All in the Family*'s refreshing crudeness, what all these shows had in common, whether done skillfully or not, was an earnestness and a determination to "do" the formerly taboo subject of homosexuality in nothing but the very best of taste.

Tastefulness certainly characterized *That Certain Summer,* the heartfelt TV-movie tale of a gay father, played by Hal Holbrook, "coming out" to his son. In fact, made-for-television movies in the early 1970s often were a prime-time showcase for both the new maturity and a new frankness about such formerly forbidden subjects as homosexuality and rape. The latter was dramatized with a hitherto unimaginable realism in both *A Case of Rape,* starring Elizabeth Montgomery, who'd so beguiled prime-time audiences in *Bewitched,* and *Born Innocent,* starring Linda Blair, best known as the demon-possessed girl in *The Exorcist,* in the fact-based story of a troubled teenager gang raped with a broom handle in reform school.

OF COURSE, PLEADING "TASTEFULNESS" WHEN DRAMATIZING controversial subjects was one way to deflect would-be censors. Take the case of *Flesh and Blood,* for example, a two-part, four-hour miniseries, based on a novel of the same name by newspaper man Pete Hamill, that aired in October of 1979 on CBS.

Like the novel, the miniseries was a *Golden Boy*-like saga of the rise from poverty of a sensitive young prizefighter, Bobby Fallon (Tom Berenger). Also like the novel, the plot featured incest between Bobby and his lonely, needy mother (Suzanne Pleshette), who'd sacrificed to raise her young son alone after being abandoned by the boy's father.

Unlike the novel, however, the TV film didn't take the viewer inside the bedroom door, bowing instead to conservative Christian pressure from a little known "watchdog" group, led by the soon-to-be famous fundamentalist minister, the Reverend Donald Wildmon, to tone the picture down.

On CBS in 1979 then, just before that fade to commercial, the viewer could find a tortured Bobby standing at his temptress mother's bedroom door, while she moves inside, murmuring, "It's all right."

"It" was most definitely left to the viewer's imagination (and familiarity with Oedipus), though later the miniseries did show mother and son in sinful Las Vegas, dancing romantically close.

Tame and melodramatic, *Flesh and Blood* nonetheless drew more than ten thousand letters of protest from Wildmon's organization, which also called for a sponsor boycott.

What made the movie and the fade-to-implied-incest bedroom scene significant was what it said about polarized public attitudes in the late 1970s. Under the avalanche of organized pressure, some sponsors caved in and withdrew, while others didn't; critics were generally underwhelmed, and the public, alerted by the furor in the press, tuned in. What made it hot for viewers less interested in "tastefulness" was a kind of mental cross-pollination: namely, the idea of incestuous sex with prim and proper Emily Hartley, Bob Newhart's TV wife.

THE SECOND HALF OF THE 1970S WAS GENERALLY A TIME OF BACK-lash when it came to popular American programming. The war in Vietnam was finally over and President Nixon had resigned in disgrace. For the first time in a decade America was at peace.

At first it seemed as if those would be the days: *All in the Family,* and such other sitcoms as *Maude* (produced, like *Family,* by

Norman Lear), had opened the door to topicality and controversy. *Maude's* forty-seven-year-old title character (Bea Arthur)
even had an abortion in 1972, before *Roe v. Wade* settled the issue
of the medical procedure's legality.

But peace in the seventies didn't mean prosperity. Instead,
seemingly, it brought an increase in public perplexity, as well as in-
flation and rising oil prices. Nixon was gone, but the forces he'd
marshaled lived on. The Christian Right was increasingly organized as the shock troops of the Silent Majority. With the Vietnam
War over, the turned-on generation tuned out, tottering out on
platform heels for night after glittery night at the disco, while fundamentalists, offended by much of "pop" culture, were not only
angry but vocal.

On TV, a wave of lesser sitcom imitators followed the seminal Lear shows, and then, perhaps inevitably, came retreat from
the cutting edge. Ostensibly concerned by the rising tide of violence in prime time, and moved by a chorus of complaints
about racy content from the no longer silent Silent Majority,
both Congress and the Federal Communications Commission
threatened action. The response from broadcasters in the mid-
seventies was predictable: a new provision in the Television
Code.

Henceforth, the new code mandated, programming between
the hours of 7 P.M. and 9 P.M. would be set aside for "family viewing." The result was cold water thrown on TV comedy's revolutionary hot talk, and the result of *that* was a brief, 5 percent drop
in primetime viewing levels for the new season.

By this time, though, Mary Richard's neighbor Phyllis had her
own spin-off show, but the punchline of the *Phyllis* pilot, set to air
in the new counter-revolutionary climate, was changed. When
the premiere was shot, Phyllis feared her teenage daughter was

having an affair, but finally concluded, "Nothing happened—if she's telling the truth." When the show aired, the last five words of the line were cut.

At *M*A*S*H,* the long-running Korean War medical comedy, the word "virgin" was deleted from one script, the word "breast" from another. And at ABC's *Barney Miller,* a sitcom set in a police station house, the idea of turning a hooker character into a continuing cast member was promptly vetoed. (It would be two decades before the short-lived *John Larroquette Show* introduced a hooker as a regular character. That 1993 sitcom about the recovering-alcoholic night manager of a seedy big-city bus station garnered generally strong reviews for a tough-minded, almost bitter sense of humor in its first season. But the ratings were low, and for its second season the show was "brightened" by network fiat, with the star getting a new upscale apartment and a girlfriend who lived across the hall, while the bus station and its seedy denizens were phased out. The ratings didn't improve, the critics took umbrage, and soon the show was canceled.)

Even *All in the Family,* the series that had started the sitcom renaissance, was affected by the mid-seventies backlash. Suddenly "inappropriate" for eight o'clock on Saturday night, where it had topped the ratings, the show was moved.

Not only talk was sanitized. A swift glimpse of bare breast might be permitted on a prestige production, but only in a "*National Geographic* context," as in background shots of bare-breasted African women in ABC's *Roots* or a bare-breasted Tahitian maiden in CBS's *Gauguin the Savage.* Otherwise it occurred only inadvertently, as when an inadequate matte shot slipped past NBC in *Captains and Kings,* a 1977 miniseries, revealing a glimpse of Beverly D'Angelo's nipple at an angle that was supposed to merely "suggest" that she was nude. Interestingly, though, not a single viewer, of the multitudes who saw it, was outraged enough to complain.[28]

PEACE HAD BROKEN OUT AT HOME, BUT IT WAS JUST ANOTHER wartime day in the Are-O-K—the Republic of Korea, that is.

As usual, Captain Benjamin Franklin "Hawkeye" Pierce (Alan Alda), the 4077's chief surgeon, is peeking in on the nurses in their shower or enticing them over to his tent—the aptly-named Swamp—for sexy banter and cocktails fresh from the doctors' very own still. But the Korean War, in the person of myopic Corporal Walter "Radar" O'Reilly (Gary Burghoff) dragging him off to the O.R., keeps intruding on his love life. And that usually gives the bemused object of his amorous affection time enough to browse through his collection of nudist magazines and dirty books.

For example, why is it, one twinkly, cheerleader-pretty blonde asks when Hawkeye finally returns from the O.R., that in his copy of *Snow White* one of the Seven Dwarfs is named Leather? And when he invites a sexy nurse for a private "wine and sleaze" party, Major Margaret "Hot Lips" Houlihan (Loretta Swit), the by-the-book chief nurse and his best foil, breaks right in on the romantic interlude, leading her entire staff and proclaiming, "Your wildest fantasy has just come true: You've been had by the whole nursing staff!"

War on *M*A*S*H* had a way of doing that. For example, there was the time the 4077's first commanding officer, forty-four-year-old Colonel Henry Blake (McLean Stevenson) went off to Tokyo for some badly needed R&R and came back enamored of Nancy Sue Parker (Kathrine Baumann), an ultra-perky twenty-year-old Air Force clerk-typist.

Henry is all ready to give up his wife back home for his cheer-leader dream girl, but no sooner does he leave her alone with Hawkeye than she throws herself into his arms and gives him an enthusiastic kiss.

"I want to thank you from the bottom of my mouth," he says, extricating himself from her embrace. Backing out, Hawkeye, never at a loss for a wisecrack, wishes a wry good night to Nancy Sue's pom-poms.

Of course, Henry sees the light and Nancy Sue heads back to Tokyo alone. Major Frank Burns (Larry Linville), a prissy moral-ist and a married man himself, is typically less than charitable about his commander's infatuation.

"A married man fooling around with another woman!" he sneers to Hot Lips, the woman with whom *he's* having an affair.

Of course, Hot Lips had her own problems with men, married and otherwise—whether it was sniveling Frank Burns, her phi-landering husband Colonel Donald Penobscot, or even General "Iron Guts" Kelly, who, in another episode, came to inspect the 4077 and died of a massive heart attack in her arms. (His aide schemed to have his body smuggled to the front to "die" glori-ously in battle.)

But no one gave her a harder time than Hawkeye, who infuri-ated her with his disrespect for the military and his shady civilian ways. Appropriately enough, it was the sheer terror of the war that finally brought them together, in a two-part 1977 episode, written and co-directed (with Burt Metcalfe) by Alda, entitled "Comrades in Arms."

On an overnight mission to the 8063, where they are to demonstrate their arterial transplant technique, Hot Lips and Hawkeye find themselves under fire and behind enemy lines. And if that isn't enough to ruin her day, Major Houlihan is also carry-

ing around an envelope that contains a letter from her husband.
The letter, however, was written to another woman—"Dear Darlene"—and it's a romantic reminiscence of their wonderful time
on the beach in Oahu.

Finally Hawkeye and Hot Lips take shelter from patrolling
enemy soldiers and constant artillery fire raining down, hiding
out in a ramshackle, abandoned hut with a thatched roof. Together they down a bottle of Japanese whiskey Hawkeye just happens to be carrying. A little tipsy, Hot Lips reads him the letter,
before they settle in for an uneasy sleep on opposite sides of the
little room. Then . . . they wake in terror to the nightmare explo-
sions of an artillery storm! The hut shakes, debris falls.

"I don't like being afraid," Margaret cries, running into Hawkeye's arms, "it scares me."

Screaming out their fears to the booming heavens, they hold
each other tighter, closer. Then as the bombs fall just outside. . . .
They kiss.

Back at the 4077, Colonel Potter (Henry Morgan), B.J. Huni-
cutt (Mike Farrell), and Father Mulcahey (William Christopher)
gather fearfully, waiting word of their missing chief surgeon and
head nurse.

"They must be going through hell out there," says B.J., as part
one ends on a cutaway to a freeze frame of Hawkeye and Hot Lips
smooching passionately.

Part two begins the next morning. Hawkeye and Hot Lips
awaken in each other's arms. She's romantic and dreamy, calling
him darling and fixing him a "continental breakfast" of crackers
and jam; he's sarcastic, calling the breakfast continental like the
continent of Atlantis, annoyed when he has to explain the joke:
"The one that sank."

And by the time they're rescued, a scene or two later, they're back to snarling at each other. "It's over," says Hawkeye of their ordeal.

"No, it isn't, buster," Margaret snaps back, "not by a long shot."

Says Hawkeye: "We got along a lot better before we started to get along."

Finally back home to a rapturous greeting by the assembled 4077, Hawkeye blurts out, "I can't tell you how glad I am you found us."

To which Hot Lips responds with a swift slap across his face.

In the episode's final scene, Hawkeye and Hot Lips, who of course looks great in her dog tags and a simple khaki T-shirt, agree to be friends and she reads him the letter she's posting back to her unfaithful husband.

Her letter, too, will be a "mistake," she says, addressed to "Dear Hank." She reads a rhapsody about a night under enemy fire, alone in an abandoned hut, the night "Hank" gave her his "warmth" because she was afraid.

In the episode's coda, with everyone sitting around the dining tent, officious Major Winchester (David Ogden Stiers) sniffs to Hawkeye and Hot Lips about their "gargantuan disaster" trapped behind enemy lines, then is puzzled by their exchange of secret smiles.

And so it went on the series that ran longer (1972–1983) than the war in which it was set.

BY THE LATE '70S, CABLE COMPANIES WERE FACING THREATS FROM irate legislators and regulators, vowing to hold *them* responsible for the "filth" on public access. *Midnight Blue,* still airing such segments as the one on which Annie Sprinkle, an exuberant porn actress making the transition to performance artist, rated various vegetables as potential sex toys and offered a guide to proper orgy etiquette, was "temporarily" suspended. The *Ugly George* show, that early mating of nonpolitically correct juvenile male obsession with the techno- and seduction possibilities of the hand-held videocam, was banned from public access as well.

Once again, self-censorship set the limits of the permissible. That was true whether it was on the Big Three networks, whose member stations were licensed after all in the public interest, or on "all-comers" public access, which originally had been nurtured by free-speech and equality advocates at the FCC, on local franchising authorities and in Congress.

No doubt they thought of it as self-preservation. All were motivated by fear of legislative or regulatory action; and of course the networks, facing organized opponents who threatened boycotts and worse, feared the loss of advertising dollars as well.

The new hit half-hour network comedies that followed in the second half of the disco decade were a throwback, in more ways than one, to the securities of an earlier time.

The show that replaced *All in the Family* at the top of the Nielsen ratings was *Laverne & Shirley,* set in the 1950s, and the producer who replaced the socially engaged Norman Lear as the king of network TV comedy was Garry Marshall, whose hallmark on both *Laverne & Shirley* and his other huge hits of the late 1970s and early eighties, *Happy Days* and *Mork & Mindy* among them, was inoffensive and shtick humor.

Happy Days took place in Milwaukee in the fifties, and the Cunninghams were a throwback to the "perfect" TV family of that era. That Laverne and Shirley (Penny Marshall and Cindy Williams), who made their first appearance on a *Happy Days* episode in which they were Richie and Fonzie's dates, were two single working-class girls who lived alone was hailed as an advance. In fact, they were originally conceived as "easy" girls and somewhat louche bimbos, but their social life always turned out to be innocent and non-realistic (i.e., non-sexual), and it was always played for pratfalls and laughs.

For example, the one time Laverne—the playgirl of the two—woke up hungover, wearing men's boxer shorts and unable to recall how she got into them, by final fadeout there turned out to be an entirely innocent explanation. She'd been given the shorts by admiring sailors she'd been carousing with, of course.

But TV sex hadn't stopped drawing viewers or selling products just because it was being criticized by conservatives and fundamentalists, or by the executive branch or in the halls of Congress, or because it was newly circumscribed by the Television Code. Topicality and controversy may have been on the wane, but double entendres and "blue" humor, basically jokey updates to the hoary farmer's daughter and traveling salesman jokes, abounded, this time with the added sizzle of tight seventies tops and hot pants.

One typically smirky sitcom was *Three's Company,* about two young women (Suzanne Somers and Joyce DeWitt) sharing their Santa Monica apartment with a young man (the prat-falling John Ritter) who pretended to be gay to foil the censorious landlord (Norman Fell). The show, ringing endless variations on this basic farcical situation, ran from the seventies through the early eighties. Its popularity was due not so much to clever writing or skilled acting (though Ritter, an expert farceur, later proved himself a fine character actor as well), but to how Chrissy Snow (Somers), a naive, big-eyed blonde, looked wrapped in a towel or dolled up in a tight top and shorts.

But the emblematic series of the period was certainly *Charlie's Angels,* an erstwhile detective series that owed its popularity to model-pretty young women with minimal acting abilities (among them Farrah Fawcett, Jaclyn Smith, Kate Jackson, Cheryl Ladd, Shelley Hack, and Tanya Roberts), who looked simply smashing in beach wear. The appeal of *Charlie's Angels,* particularly for young men, was captured succinctly by one word, and that word was "jiggle."

Soap, a prime-time sitcom satire of the daytime genre, was, arguably, one mild counterweight to the throwback trend. Before debuting in the fall of 1977, the sitcom had the good fortune of being lambasted by the Reverend Donald Wildmon and thereby reaped a windfall of pre-premiere publicity. His Tupelo, Mississippi-based National Federation for Decency, a conservative Christian media watchdog group, organized a letter-writing campaign to ABC that resulted in more than thirty thousand letters opposing *Soap's* supposed "frank" sexuality, particularly that of one regular character, Jodie Dallas, an effete gay man who wanted a sex-change operation (he was played by Billy Crystal, then an unknown).

But that turned out to be an overstatement. Even so, both the Jodie character, who became less flamboyant and gave up ambitions for a sex change, and the general tenor of the show were toned down in response to Wildmon's threatened sponsor boycott. On *Soap,* too, satire regularly gave way to simple shtick, and all that it turned out to offer was the usual smarmy smirk and contrived plots that left reality far behind.

ALL OF THESE SHOWS, FROM GARRY MARSHALL'S *LAVERNE & Shirley* to Aaron Spelling's *Charlie's Angels,* were regularly among the most-watched programs on American TV in the second half of the 1970s and early '80s. All of them, with the qualified exception of *Soap,* were regularly derided by the critics. And all had one other thing in common: They all aired on ABC, historically the

third-ranked network, but the first to make a demographic appeal
to advertisers, arguing that its shows "skewed" younger because
they were racier, and that young viewers were more valuable to
advertisers, who should pay a premium for airing commercials on
the series that appealed to them.

That argument is conventional wisdom today, in our multi-
channel universe of "narrowcasting" to fragmented audiences,
when advertisers regularly pay higher prices to air commercials on
shows that reach young people (and particularly young men),
who are presumed to have more disposable income and be more
prone to advertising's seductive suasions. But, at first, "demographics" was a controversial concept and a hard sell, derided as
selling "sizzle" by the men who ran CBS and NBC, which specialized in selling the "steak" of the mass audience.

In any event, with those and similar shows as the backbone of
its schedule, ABC captured not only younger audiences, but larger
audiences, too, shocking its complacent competitors by swiftly rising to first place in the ratings.

Dagmar's Charms: Members of Congress viewed them with shock and alarm; then as now, most of the country was happy just to watch.

From Vampira to Buffy (Sarah
Michelle Gellar) and Angel
(David Boreanaz): There's always been something sexy
about TV's Undead.

Loving Lucy: Even in the 1950s, many Americans understood that this could conceivably lead to that.

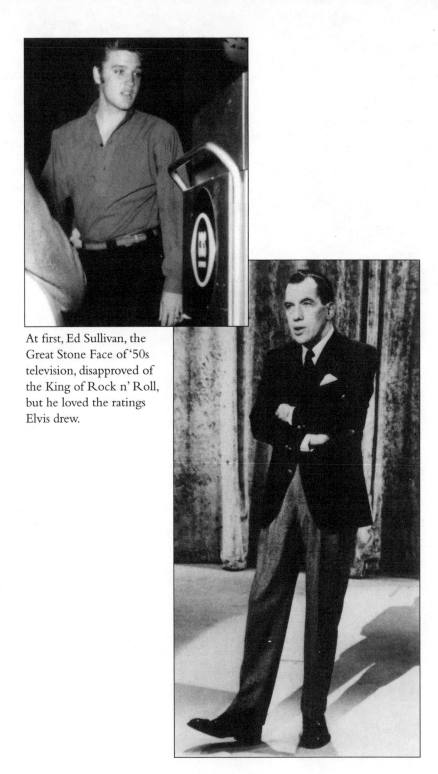

At first, Ed Sullivan, the Great Stone Face of '50s television, disapproved of the King of Rock n' Roll, but he loved the ratings Elvis drew.

Gunsmoke was an "adult" Western, but just try telling that to Miss Kitty (Amanda Blake), alone in the tub again.

The tenor of the TV times, circa 1960: (from left) Jack Paar, host of "The Tonight Show"; his sidekick, Hugh Downs; and Jose Melis, the show's band-leader.

Peyton Place, the original prime-time soap: Innocent Alison MacKenzie (Mia Farrow) worked in the bookstore owned by her mother, Constance (Dorothy Malone).

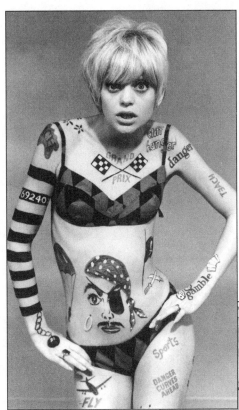

Navel Battles: Jeannie wasn't allowed to have one; Goldie Hawn, on Laugh-In, painted hers.

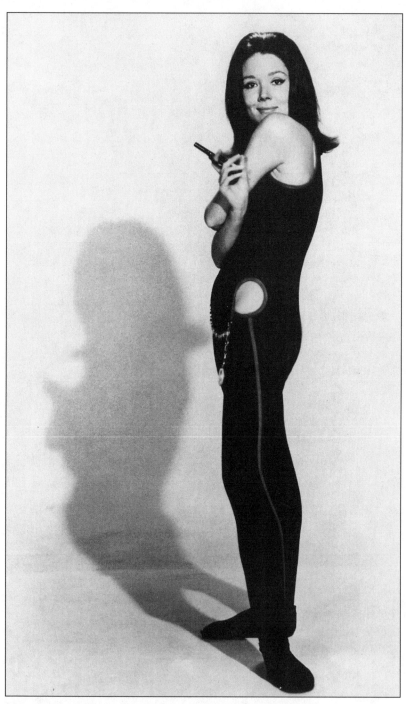

Mrs. Emma Peel (Diana Rigg) on The Avengers: Read her name as "M. Appeal," shorthand for "Male Appeal."

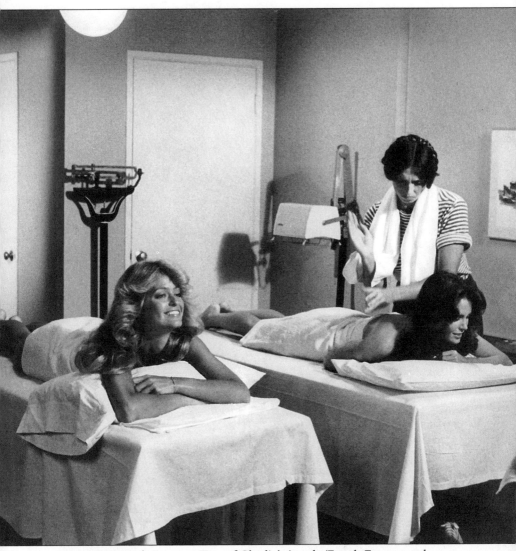

Private Eyes With Bounce: Two of Charlie's Angels (Farrah Fawcett and Jaclyn Smith), undercover at a health spa. The masseuse was played by actress Janis Jamison.

Luke (Anthony Geary) and Laura (Genie Francis) on General Hospital:
From rape to romance to daytime's Wedding of the Decade.

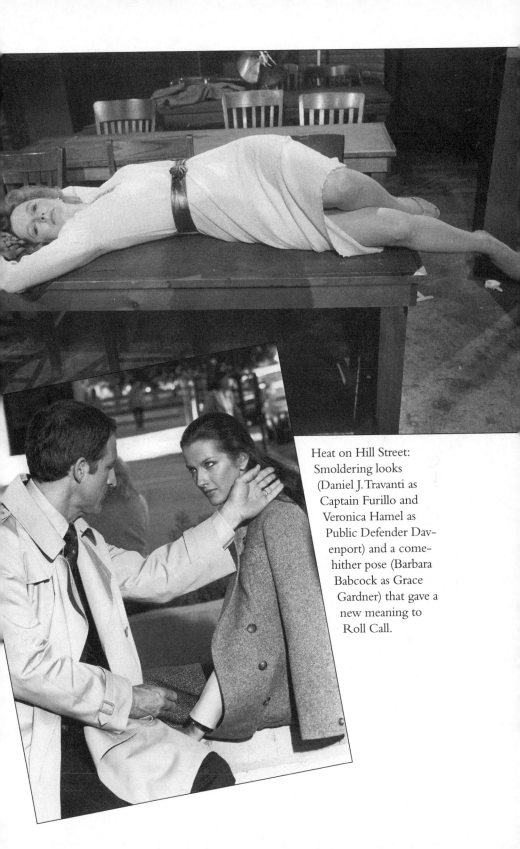

Heat on Hill Street: Smoldering looks (Daniel J. Travanti as Captain Furillo and Veronica Hamel as Public Defender Davenport) and a come-hither pose (Barbara Babcock as Grace Gardner) that gave a new meaning to Roll Call.

Freeze, Miami Vice: The coolest cast on '80s TV posing for a publicity pic.

Tracy (aka, Traci) Lords, America's scandalous underage porn star, played "Vanessa Van Pelt" in the Married . . . With Children episode entitled "Al Bundy, Shoe Dick." A mid-'80s porn scandal didn't kill her chance for a mainstream career; instead, she went on to guest star on Roseanne, Melrose Place, Nash Bridges, Profiler, and others.

Whether it was sex, drugs or rock 'n roll, Eddie (Jennifer Saunders) and Patsy (Joanna Lumley) were Absolutely Fabulous.

Witty dialogue and Helen Hunt made Mad About You madly sexy.

From Ellen's enormously hyped and debated coming-out episode: Ellen De-
Generes and Laura Dern, who played Susan, Ellen's first lesbian love interest.

Disorder In the Court: Ally (Calista Flockhart) and Cage (Peter MacNicol) share a romantic dance in Ally McBeal, the Boston lawyer series in which every case seems to be about sex.

Can you find the gay role model in this picture? The Reverend Jerry Falwell could.

Before the Big Break-Up: Sex and the City's resident "sexpert" Carrie Bradshaw (Sarah Jessica Parker) and Mr. Big (Chris Noth), the man of her dreams.

What would Congressman Gathers have said? . . . Jennifer Lopez, setting a new standard in plunging necklines (and in the process making every TV newscast in the land), at the 2000 Grammys.

Who is Cartman's dad? From the South Park episode entitled "Cartman's Mom Is a Dirty Slut," here's little Eric himself with some of the many suspects.

Dolled up at the 2000 Oscars . . . A South Park trio: (from left) Trey Parker (the voice of Stan, Eric, Mr. Garrison and others), wearing a Jennifer Lopez-style dress; Marc Shaiman, who cowrote the Oscar-nominated song "Blame Canada" for South Park: Bigger, Longer and Uncut, the show's film version; and Matt Stone (the voice of Kyle and Kenny, among others), channeling Gwyneth Paltrow.

The Eighties

Hill Street, *Cheers,* Bickering
P.I.s, and MTV Cops

AS THE 1980S DAWNED, THERE WAS FIFTEEN-YEAR-OLD BROOKE
Shields (who'd played a prepubescent prostitute in Louis Malle's
daring *Pretty Baby*), a teenage model and actress with an erotic
gleam in her eye, proclaiming that nothing came between her and
her Calvins—her Calvin Klein jeans, that is. It was sexy, it was
scandalous, and it was a commercial airing on network prime time.

TELEVISION IS A CYCLICAL BUSINESS AND TV SERIES HAVE LIFE CY-
cles. By the early 1980s, ABC's smirky sitcom hits had grown tired
and it fell from the top of the greasy ratings pole. But the network's
programmers didn't strike out in a new direction. Instead, they fell
back on the type of programming that had worked before, debuting a veritable Jello bowl of jiggle shows—series like *It's a Living,*
about (nubile) waitresses at an ersatz Playboy Club, *Too Close For
Comfort,* about a single father (Ted Knight, the stentorian-voiced
Ted Baxter on the old *Mary Tyler Moore Show*) living in the apart-

ment above his two (nubile) adult daughters, and *Bosom Buddies,* about two guys dressing in drag (one was Tom Hanks, the other Peter Scolari) in order to live at a hotel catering exclusively to (nubile) young women. Generally, the shows failed.

And in Hollywood, at studio commissaries and over expense account lunches, a conventional wisdom coalesced: the half-hour situation-comedy genre was dead.

"LET'S GET OUT THERE AN' DO IT TO THEM BEFORE THEY DO IT to us."

That was the exhortation that ended every morning roll call at the Hill Street station house, but it may as well have been the motto at NBC when it first began to air *Hill Street Blues* (1981–1987).

After all, the proud Peacock Network was in a rating tailspin, and neither the viewers nor the critics would have been surprised to see it sink into something like perpetual third place. So perhaps it's not surprising that this was the network willing to take a chance on an unconventional show, one with an edgy new style.

One of the most influential, though far from the highest-rated, shows of the period, *Blues,* created by Michael Kozoll and Steven Bochco, pushed the edge of the permissible, with multiple story lines, more daring language ("Butt face," a cop calls a crooked health inspector as he arrests him), and a swooping, restless, hand-held camera style. It also said something new and realistic about contemporary relationships.

In one 1981 episode, for example, Captain Frank Furillo (Daniel J. Travanti) and prosecutor Joyce Davenport (Veronica Hamill) are shown in a bathtub together, albeit at opposite ends of the tub. Frequently, subsequent episodes faded out with them in bed, reviewing their day, cuddling, trading mildly suggestive remarks, as in the episode which ends with Joyce picking crumbs off Furillo's bare chest before climbing on top of him and "checking for bruises."

The complicated relationships between men and women, and the issues of the day, their complexities intact, were regular fare for *Hill Street*. In one controversial episode, for example, a militant abortion protester is overcome with remorse after he inadvertently knocks a pregnant woman down, causing her miscarriage, while he's throwing blood on an abortion doctor.

In another episode, recently separated Chief Fletcher Daniels (Jon Cypher) crudely propositions a pretty female cop, Detective Patsy Mayo (Mimi Kuzyk), whom he's pressured to go out on a date. The next day, he publicly and loudly accuses her of being a coward because she won't be "bait" for a serial killer who's decapitated seven prostitutes. (The hooker-hacking serial killer plot is something of a fixture in cop shows of the past two decades.)

"Little tramp," the chief whispers under his breath when Captain Furillo takes her side later on.

"Gangland tramp," Fay Furillo (Barbara Bosson), whispers in yet another episode, in which Mrs. Gina Srignoli (Jennifer Tilly, in one of her earliest gangland-bimbo-with-a-brain roles) is carrying on a torrid affair with mild-mannered Lieutenant Henry Goldblume (Joe Spano).

"That's beneath you," says Goldblume, who's overheard her.

"We all know what's beneath *you*," she shoots back.

Typically, sensitive Captain Furillo both understands his smitten lieutenant's lust and Chief Daniels' "wounded vanity," which he forces the chief to face. The chief duly recants, regretting his "shoddy advances" and takes Officer Mayo aside, apologizes, saying, tellingly, "This damn sex business between men and women— it really mucks things up."

Yes indeed, and in a way that dramatists historically, from the Greek poets forward, have been pleased to depict. At an intimate dinner that night, just before the lovers go home, Joyce offers to give Captain Furillo's ego a "boost," and there's no mistaking what she's talking about.

It's not just Officer John "J.D." La Rue's ego either that gets swollen in the episode in which he goes from getting involved in a home-security video to starring in a porn shoot—urged on by the shady producer (played by Brent Spiner, best known for his role as Data on *Star Trek: The Next Generation*).

Trying to assuage J.D.'s nerves on the set before their big scene, Lulu (Patti Tippo), a hard-bitten, cigarette-puffing young blonde in a white bathrobe, tells him of her first time. It was "one of those multiple person scenarios," she says, using an acceptable circumlocution for "orgy scene." Then, offering to show him exactly what he'll be working with, she stands in front of him, her back to the camera, and drops her robe. Her bare back and his appreciative and astounded look fill the screen. From this shot, the mid-eighties scene, controversial in its time, fades to black.

Turning toward or away from the camera at the crucial point, usually to depict nudity without showing it explicitly, became the strategy of choice at *Hill Street* and other series that followed. In fact, an episode or two after the porn shoot, Furillo comes into possession of the video, viewing it with J.D. (Kiel Martin), who swears that it isn't him in the hard-core shots.

He'd gone there, sure, he admits, but then he changed his mind. They used a double, he tells Captain Furillo—you only see him when his back is to the camera, and they intercut it with shots of J.D. wearing his raincoat. See, says J.D., pointing at the screen, which Furillo is watching (but we don't see it), he's got a tattoo and I don't.

Furillo plainly doesn't believe him, but he's willing to let the matter drop. He gets up, heads for the door, when J.D. cries out "This is my career!" as he stands, facing the camera, while pulling at his belt. "Now, you take a look!"

As he bends toward us, he drops his trousers. "The defense rests."

Meanwhile, elsewhere...

Even in conservative Italy, innuendo and "jiggle" are the order of the day on television, too, so a group of video-minded Italian feminists decides to strike back...with a daring documentary!

They hire a pretty, twenty-five-year-old French prostitute named Veronique La Croix, import her to Rome, set her up in a flat, and place the requisite "masseuse" advertisements in the local newspapers. Then, with video cameras hidden behind a two-way mirror in her bedroom, they record everything that transpires.

The resulting footage is sold to a national Italian television network and edited into a 90-minute documentary, complete with steamy—but not explicit—footage of the prostitute and her clients, including one who begs to be whipped and another who threatens her with a gun.

But just one day before it's set to air, powerful ruling-party politicians condemn the project, calling it—gasp!—pornography. The network, RAI-TV, is state-owned, and politico-

continued on next page

continued from previous page

controlled, and really has no choice: The show is shelved and
Veronique's amorous Roman adventure never airs.

One morning, some two decades later, RAI mistakenly airs
an American soft-core porn movie. Even as irate viewers phone
in to complain, the show's ratings shoot up while the broadcast
continues. Halfway through, however, an executive orders it off
the air. The problem, according to an RAI statement, was that
the picture had been mislabeled.[29] Given the latest trend in international television, the executive might have done better to
replace the inadvertent porn with the Veronique tape.

THE 1980S WERE THE REAGAN YEARS—A RESTORATION AFTER
two decades of often chaotic social change. It was morning in
America again, as his campaign slogan characterized it. The Reagan era brought deregulation and merger mania, and in 1983, after
a federal court ruled that some of its provisions violated the Sher-
man Antitrust Act, the end of the National Association of Broadcasters' Code for both radio and television. It ushered in the
triumph of Wall Street, the greed-is-good ethic, and free market
capitalism. It was the Age of the yuppie. It was also the plague-
years Era of AIDS, and the "Just Say No" years, too.

Political winds in the United States are said to blow from the
(liberal) left or from the (conservative) right, but, ironically, the
prevailing philosophical zephyr of the Reagan years also ended up
blowing down his conservative allies' most-treasured family-
friendly broadcasting regulation—the family hour itself.

Deregulation also meant to the nation's broadcasters that, finally, they had less to fear from possible government intervention.

Gradually it dawned on the producers, too, that fewer people were watching over their shoulders while they went about the business of creating network TV programming.

Media proliferated in the 1980s. Cable spread its web of wires to cities, small towns, and suburbs alike, while the VCR and video rental business, which has since become bigger than the movies themselves, took off for the stratosphere. And hardcore pornography, the original made-for-video genre, led the way, also becoming a multi billion dollar industry. Of course, porn has a trade organization, too, and as the eighties churned along it changed its name from the Adult Film Association to the Adult Film and Video Association to, finally, the Adult Video Association.

Centered in the Los Angeles area's sprawling San Fernando Valley, the porn business mirrors traditional Hollywood in more ways than one. Often the very same techies—the shooters and cutters, the sound and lighting people—who toil for the studios and networks by day pick up extra money under the table churning out porno tapes by night.

By the early 1980s, both *Midnight Blue* and *Ugly George* were back on New York public access, and cable had launched at least six "premium pay" networks that showed nothing but sexually explicit programming—with titles like *Wild and Willing, Lonely Wives,* and *Captain Lust.*

Social critics of television, many of them traditionalists and fundamentalists opposed to the "new immorality," were proliferating, too. Attempts to legislate bans on cable "obscenity," in localities as various as Utah and Florida, were generally struck down by the courts as unconstitutional. Ironically, the well-publicized opposition to cable "porn" often resulted in a rush of curious new subscribers, attracted by the furor. But the critics also hastened the advent of key-operated "channel lockout" boxes, which allowed

parents to protect children from the new explicitness. But broadcast television, still the only one with an all-encompassing
national reach, still totally dependent on advertising revenue, remained the critics' primary target.

According to one estimate, by the early eighties at least 130 organized special-interest groups were trying to influence the content of network television.[30] They were forming alliances and
associations, too. As the eighties began, the Tupelo, Mississippi-
based Reverend Donald Wildmon joined forces with the Lynch-
burg, Virginia-based Reverend Jerry Falwell, the founder of the
Moral Majority. And even though sitcom social criticism, à la
Norman Lear, and jiggle shows, à la Aaron Spelling, were both
down sharply, Wildmon and Falwell vowed to monitor programming and boycott sponsors of "morally offensive" shows.

One of Wildmon's first targets was an unassuming little NBC
comedy with drama called *Love, Sidney,* starring Tony Randall as
Sidney Shorr, a lachrymose art director who begins sharing his
antique-filled eight-room Manhattan apartment with a young aspiring actress who is a single mother-to-be. Though the point
wasn't made explicitly, Sidney, who loved old Greta Garbo films
and displayed a framed photograph on his mantle of a handsome
man who was not his brother, was "understood" to be a closeted
gay man. This early example of the hybrid form known as "dramedy" was played innocently and circumspectly, and often sweetly.
It was, nonetheless, a forerunner of such broadly played sitcoms as
Will & Grace, the often hilarious NBC series about a gay man
rooming with a straight woman.

THE TRADITIONAL BIG THREE BROADCAST NETWORKS WERE
under attack by the old, culturally conservative critics of the New
Right, which was newly empowered by its role in the Reagan

Revolution, as well as by the new competition, generally free from content restrictions and growing stronger all the time. The traditional three networks fought back with glitz and glitter, in a succession of prime-time one-hour soaps chronicling the gilded lives and heavy-breathing, high-stakes machinations of the extended families of the super rich.

It was a formula that tended to veer into camp and, of course, the main ingredient was sex. On *Dynasty,* for example, oil mogul Blake Carrington's son Steven apparently switched from gay to straight, from season to season, his sexual orientation entirely a function of the needs of the plot.

It was the era of *Dallas* (1978–1991) and J.R. Ewing, *Dynasty* (1981–1989) and the epic good versus evil contest between Krystle (Linda Evans), the blonde ice queen, and Alexis (Joan Collins), the scheming, raven-haired temptress. It was the era, too, of *Falcon Crest* (1981–1990), set in California's wine country, and such lesser entries as *Flamingo Road* (set in Florida's political swamps), and *Paper Dolls* (set in the world of Manhattan models). The latter three all starred Morgan Fairchild, big-haired, leggy, and blonde, one of the emblematic prime-time TV "vixens" of the Me Decade, who specialized in characters that exuded calculation and ambition.

Back in daytime, couples, adulterous and otherwise, routinely *talked* about "making love," but when it came to scripts that used the phrases "doing it," "having sex," or even "going to bed," the censor's red pencil was still apt to intrude.

Of course by this time, when it came to program formats, whatever the broadcast networks could do the new cable networks could do, too—if not better, then at least with fewer clothes. This point was demonstrated by *A New Day in Eden,* Showtime's 1982–1983 nighttime soap, which had topless coeds, lesbian love scenes, and nudes cavorting in the shower.

BY THE MID-EIGHTIES, THE BROADCAST NETWORKS HAD ALSO DIS-
covered the viewer appeal of bold-themed TV movies that rightly
treated controversial subjects as the "social problems" they were.
Those subjects included battered wives (*The Burning Bed,* 1984,
which marked Farah Fawcett's transformation from *Angel* to actress), incest (*Something About Amelia,* 1984), AIDS (*An Early Frost,*
1985), and sex-change surgery and discrimination against trans-
sexuals (*Second Serve,* 1986). The movies were prestigious and attracted A-list players (Ted Danson and Glenn Close in *Amelia;*
Ben Gazzara and Gena Rowlands in *Frost;* and Vanessa Redgrave
as Richard who becomes Renee in *Serve*).

The Big Three broadcast networks had discovered they could
talk about anything, even if they couldn't show everything. The
broadcast networks were still doing well financially, but their
once vast audience, no longer their sole monopoly, was beginning to shrink.

First to desert the networks were the grown-up Boomers'
cable-ready kids who wanted their MTV. Over at the wildly successful twenty-four-hour music video channel the prevailing
ethos was summarized succinctly early on by one video director
as "blue screens, smoke machines and chicks." And as it happened,
it was precisely those MTV-mad kids—the Madonna-wannabes
and the teenage boys lusting after them—with all that disposable
income, that the advertisers most wanted to reach.

Precisely which story lines and which visual "hooks" attracted younger viewers was something the daytime soaps had
always instinctively understood: When summer rolled around,
and all those kids were out of school and in front of the set, the
soap plots would heat up, and there would be more skimpy
swimming-suit scenes.

Network programmers pondered and pondered and came up

with ... *MTV Cops!*—which, as the famous, perhaps apocryphal story has it, was what NBC's Brandon Tartikoff scribbled down on a napkin at one business lunch. In the hands of producers the programmer's napkin turned into the pluperfect eighties series—a vivid and colorful melange of sun, sex, cocaine, rock and roll, and a soft-spoken and soulful narcotics cop hero who was perfectly tanned and wore pastel designer threads, but owned nary a single pair of socks. The show was called *Miami Vice.*

"FREEZE, MIAMI VICE!"

Then would come the gunfire and the bodies, usually in slow motion, falling in counterpoint to the throbbing beat. Cool Sonny Crockett and his partner, dapper Ricardo Tubbs—cops in a pastel-drenched night world who walked the walk right up to, and sometimes right over, the line.

At its best, the emblematic eighties series (1984–1989) conjured up the sweaty, pulsing feverishness of Miami's narco-cowboys and the cool intensity of the stylish vice-squad cops who pursued them—in water-skimming cigarette boats or at the wheel of a throaty Ferrari, and sometimes even on foot.

The series was relentlessly hip (Glenn Frey, Phil Collins, Iggy Pop, Frank Zappa, and Miles Davis were among the real-life musicians who guest starred on single episodes). Its existential, Armani-clad heroes haunted the clubs and the night spots and helped to make South Beach fashionable. Like cops shows before it set in tropical locales such as Hawaii, it had the advantage of not needing excuses to shoot scenes with pretty girls in tiny bathing suits, their navels and much more very visible.

Even so, the series turned up the heat of what was casually, perhaps even gratuitously, permissible, specializing in loving, close-up pans along tanned, sunscreen-slathered legs or spicing up a crime scene with a bullet-spattered body in a bikini, splayed decoratively in the background.

Where once upon a time, in the early days, a plunging neckline might "inadvertently" plunge too far to partially expose a breast on live TV, giving a starlet invaluable publicity, *Vice*'s brief, playful exposure of a bare-breasted woman was clearly intended—and was never made much of by producers or even particularly remarked upon by the press.

"Trust Fund Pirates," a 1986 episode, guest starred Richard Belzer as Captain Hook, an eye-patch-wearing, rap-spouting DJ, who broadcasts offshore, from a pirate radio ship. At the beginning of the episode, hip-hop Hook introduces a Randy Newman song. The camera cuts away to a long shot of a sunny beach.

Walking toward us is a blonde, just slightly out of focus, in a one-piece suit cut high to show off her long legs. She's just risen out of the water and the top of her suit is down, near the bottom of her breasts, and despite the soft focus we can see her nipples. As she pulls up on the top of the suit, the focus of the shot sharpens right along with her motion. She comes closer while Randy Newman, best known perhaps for singing "L.A.... we love it," rhapsodizes nasally about the joys of Miami.

That episode also contains a scene in a neon-lighted nightclub so trendy that the wall decorations are Andy Warhol-like Pop Art representations of *I Love Lucy*. It guest stars Tom Chong, part of the Cheech and Chong drug humor duo of the seventies and eighties, as Jumbo, a fence for stolen goods. (Chong nowadays turns up on *That '70s Show*. His former partner, Cheech Marin, plays Joe, the sidekick on *Nash Bridges,* Don Johnson's late-nineties cop series, set in San Francisco. That series airs on Friday, in *Vice*'s old time period, but, as the promotional tag goes, on another network.)

Miami Vice aired on the one night when dateless kids were

(and are still) presumed to be in front of the set. This made *Vice's* heady mix of sex for sale, drug dealing for narcodollars, anti-anticommunist politics, MTV-like musical montages and, not least, moments of slow motion, choreographed violence all the more striking, especially when it was done well.

Which it most certainly was in the mid-eighties episode entitled "Duty and Honor" (also known as "The Savage"), directed by the late John Nicolella.

It's the seamy, steamy story of a psychopathic serial killer, who, in a prologue set in the early seventies during the Vietnam War, begins to kill prostitutes in Saigon. The killer's bloody murder spree extends over a decade and a half, leaving long-haired brunette hookers dead from Bangkok to Copenhagen, to Brussels, to Paris, to Nicaragua and finally to Miami, all killed with the same military knife.

Adding gravitas to this story are the late Dr. Haing S. Ngor, as a former Saigon cop with a secret, and Edward James Olmos, in his recurring role of Lieutenant Martin Castillo, black-suited and mustachioed, pocked and brooding, the taciturn head of Miami Vice.

He's been haunted by the killer since he was a military policeman and first came across the bloody body of a prostitute with the words *VC* (for Viet Cong) *Whore* scrawled in blood on a brothel wall.

Ngor, an Oscar winner for his heartfelt performance in *The Killing Fields*, plays the former Saigon policeman named Tranh, and he turns up on the killer's trail when the murders begin in Miami.

Soon we see the murderer. A thin, intense black man in a long black leather coat regards himself in a mirror. Reaching up to brush a hand through his hair, he whips the knife out from its sheath between his shoulder blades. In a montage over rock music, we see him drive away, pick up a street hooker, and later, bare-chested, he walks menacingly toward her, the deadly blade in his hand.

Still later, the hard-working Vice cops come up with a list of hooker killings in cities around the world...murders that were always followed by the assassination of a Communist or suspected Communist. Such a man—a Latin American political figure, guarded by a private security firm headed by a brush cut former CIA agent—happens to be in Miami at that moment to give a speech.

The killer, Castillo learns from his own CIA contact, had taken part in a covert assassination program in Vietnam called Operation Phoenix (such an operation actually existed) and was known by a code name: the Savage.

Meanwhile, from a Vietnam vet Crockett hears a "wild story," that the Savage's killings began after a prostitute, who was secretly a V.C. operative, emasculated him in an assassination attempt. Still later, the cops find out that the Savage's one-time "handler" is now the private security head guarding the Latin politico. Castillo and Tranh race to stop the Savage, who wounds Castillo before Tranh kills him.

Tranh picks up the knife as we cut to another hotel room, where the security agent/ex-CIA handler is assuring someone on the telephone that they have nothing to fear, because the Savage will never allow himself to be taken alive.

The door opens, Tranh stands there silently, and with a quick throw of the Savage's own knife, kills the agent/handler. Then he disappears and we learn that Tranh, too, was not what he seemed: the "Saigon policeman" is actually a colonel in the North Vietnamese Army.

Operatic? Overwrought? Certainly, and often over the top, too.

It was grim business, this *Vice* episode linking sex and violence, leavened only by a first-act cameo by British actress Helena Bonham Carter, whom (*Fight Club* notwithstanding) we are more accustomed to seeing in period costume, complete with bustle, in Merchant and Ivory films.

She turns up here as Dr. Theresa Lyons, wearing only a sheet, on the bed in Sonny Crockett's houseboat. He's standing beside her, shirtless, and he's just gotten off the telephone.

"Do you get many phone calls at precisely *that* moment?" she asks prettily.

Sonny shrugs it off. A bad habit, this taking telephone calls while making love, but what can be done?

Says Dr. Lyons, pulling up the sheet to reveal her bare feet: "I prescribe, um, convulsive muscular therapy."

That was sexy, but sexiest of all (and for a very particular reason) has to be "By Hooker by Crook," with a story by Dick Wolf, the *Vice* producer who went on to create *Law and Order*, among other series. The 1987 episode, in which Melanie Griffith, Don Johnson's ex-wife, guest starred, was directed by Johnson himself. The two had a real-life history that easily could have been turned into a TV movie, too.

By the time Don Johnson was nineteen, he'd been in a juvenile detention center, gone on to college, acted with the American Conservatory Theater, made his film debut, and been married twice (both marriages were annulled).

He was twenty-one when he met fourteen-year-old Melanie Griffith on the set of *The Harrad Experiment*, starring her mother, actress Tippi Hedren. A year later, she started living with him. Three years later, they eloped to Las Vegas. Six months after that, they were divorced.

They were poster children for troubled show business youth;

their relationships with other people, and their troubles with alcohol and drugs, were well chronicled by the tabloids. In 1983,
Johnson completed a treatment program for substance abuse. In
1988, Griffith went into rehab for alcoholism. In 1989, they re-
married in Aspen. Subsequently, of course, they divorced yet again
and Griffith married the actor Antonio Banderas. But it was in
'87, before the remarriage and second divorce, before the alcoholism rehab, that they reunited on the small screen.

Melanie played Christine Von Marburg, a well-connected busi-
nesswoman raised in wealth and privilege, who turns out to be
the madam of an upscale call-girl ring. Also guest starring in the
episode were George Takei (Mr. Sulu in the original *Star Trek*), as
a languid, sushi-eating criminal mastermind who surrounds himself with artfully lighted tanks of tropical fish, and Vanity, a TV and
movie actress, as Christine's favorite hooker, Ali Ferrand, who has
the misfortune to witness a murder.

Of course, Sonny and Christine "meet cute," obviously smitten with each other, at a charity ball. She tries to guess his pro-
fession and comes up with jewel thief, traveling evangelist, "or
maybe a gigolo," while he can't get over the fact that this beautiful woman also reads Shakespeare and has a fondness for both
post-Impressionist art and Buddy Holly.

He calls her front door the Berlin Wall after their first date,
when she won't let him come in. But by then the real wall was
only two years away from coming down, and in the saga of Sonny
and Christine their wall falls the very next night.

They're in her penthouse apartment, bantering. "Anything I
can do for you?" Christine asks, as Sonny takes her in his arms.

"If pressed I could come up with something," Sonny replies, as
we dissolve into a montage of the two making love—a tangle of
bare limbs, a quick side view of a bare breast, Melanie's bare back

as she strains upward—while on the soundtrack Steve Winwood sings about the "High Life."

But because this is *Miami Vice*, inevitably the sex is intercut with picturesque violence: Ali being caught and strangled to death by two hulking hoods.

By 1987 TV had developed a convention for showing a heterosexual couple, ostensibly nude, in bed—the actress wearing a flesh-colored body stocking and the actor in shorts. But Don and Melanie, in a triumph of either friskiness or method acting, actually did do it in this sexy sex scene, according to insider whispers at the time.

As the rest of the plot unfolds, Sonny is devastated to learn his new paramour is a brothel madam in league with a criminal mastermind. But Christine agrees to wear a wire to help bring the evil crook to justice, and in the process Sonny hears her having sex with him. Later, in the mandatory final slow motion shootout, with tropical fish tanks shattering everywhere, it's Christine herself who plugs the evil mastermind. Sonny gets the charges against her dropped and, in return, Christine Von Marburg agrees to leave the country, but not before a heartfelt and pointed denunciation, with real-life echoes, of the crusading publisher and the TV station executive—clients both—who'd editorialized hypocritically against her immoral ways.

THE OTHER SEMINAL (AND SEXY) SERIES OF THE PERIOD WAS *Moonlighting* (1985–1989), an hour "dramedy" set in the Blue Moon Detective Agency and starring Bruce Willis and Cybill Shepherd, as David Addison (a wisecracking working-class sexist) and Maddie Hayes (an elegant uppercrust ex-model, with cool Grace Kelly looks), a most mismatched pair of private eyes. "Ham and Legs," the writers breezily summarized the duo in one episode.

A full decade before *Ally McBeal*, *Moonlighting* was depicting its characters' interior lives with fantasy sequences—Ray Charles, for example, turning up complete with piano and back-up singers in David's living room to sing love-life advice to the tune of "Georgia on My Mind."

At its best, the show was more about style and a stylish deconstruction of the traditional one-hour genre than it was about cracking cases and catching the bad guys. Willis and Shepherd regularly broke the so-called fourth wall by talking, in character, directly to the audience, often remarking on the "action" and the quality of the show's writing.

At the end of one episode, for example, when their late client's lawyer, his villainy unmasked, flees, Maddie immediately asks, "David, you know what this means?"

"I sure do," he replies enthusiastically, with a sidelong glance. "Start the chase music, boys!" And Willis and the villain proceed to fight it out with mops, while the stirring light-saber-duel music from *Star Wars* plays.

In another episode ("Camille"), guest starring Whoopi Goldberg, Judd Nelson, and (in a small part) David Paymer, the chase runs right off the set and right out of sound stage 20 on the Fox back lot, with the villain (Nelson) stopping to ask a passing cowboy on a horse if he's a good guy or bad guy.

"Bad guy," says the cowboy laconically. "Me, too," the villain declares, hopping up on the horse for a ride. And as they gallop away, with David and the ever-screeching Maddie in pursuit, the rousing music from *The Magnificent Seven* accompanies the chase.

There were also spoofs (of *Poltergeist* and *It's A Wonderful Life*, among others), elaborate musical and dance numbers, and a black-and-white homage to forties film noir. And there were such offbeat episodes as the retrospective "clip" show in which Rona

Barrett (an actual eighties gossip columnist), "invades" the Blue
Moon offices with a camera crew, searching out the real dirt
about rumors that Maddie and David aren't getting along. (In
"real" life by then, the tabloids were rife with speculation that
Shepherd and Willis loathed each other and that *Moonlighting* was
a "troubled" set.)

Perhaps the most celebrated *Moonlighting* episode of all, though,
was the comic take-off on *The Taming of the Shrew*—an entire
episode (entitled "Atomic Shakespeare") in period costume, with
sunglasses provided for both Willis *and* his horse, and with all the
characters declaiming in iambic pentameter!

Outside of the sexy will-they-won't-they banter, though, and
the few episodes that so famously departed from the formula, it
all began to seem a little too familiar—the perfidious client
who's conning Maddie and David (or its variant, the client
who's being conned, usually by a treacherous lover, and ends up
dead); the Greek chorus of Blue Moon employees, oohing and
aahing in the background, in unison; Miss DiPesto's rhymes; the
obligatory madcap chase in the final moments, during which
Maddie, clutching a purse and whooping and shrieking, is tied
up in a wheelchair or dumped upside down in a mail cart, long
legs flapping, or is otherwise humiliated, while David, forever
smirking, pushes or pulls her in pursuit of the unmasked villain.
And then, finally, at the end of its second season...the show
launched an arc of episodes built around Maddie's affair with
Sam Crawford (Mark Harmon), her childhood friend who grew
up to be an astronaut.

"Dish city," says Miss DiPesto dreamily when she first sees him.
And it's David's jealousy over this turn that prompts his growing
realization that he's in love with his partner.

All the while, as the story line unfolded, the show continued to joke about its stars' well-publicized antipathy toward each other and its own annoying failure to deliver new episodes to the once-loyal fans.

In the final moments of the arc's big finale ("I Am Curious... Maddie," the last episode of the second season), with the sparks between the two lead actors obviously guttering, Maddie and David do it, accompanied by the thumping beat and teen-lust lyrics of the emblematic sixties Girl Group song, "Be My Baby," sung by Ronnie Spector.

Moonlighting's next season was an evolving disaster. Sex with Maddie, it turned out, was better even than David had ever imagined. But she became distant and "ambivalent," and finally fled to her parents' home in Chicago. He pined—lovelorn, nervous, and desperate—pursuing her as ardently as any teenager, even declaring his love in front of the Blue Moon Greek chorus.

The sparkly flirting was gone. In episode after episode the two leads didn't share a single scene. The show's creator, Glenn Gordon Caron (who went on to create *Now and Again* for CBS) was forced out—by Shepherd, according to reports at the time. *Die Hard* made Willis a movie star. Cybill's real-life pregnancy was written into the series, but it only served to highlight her absences and the two stars' alienation. What had worked for Lucy was a fiasco for *Moonlighting*, even ending sourly with an episode in which Maddie has a miscarriage. (In fantasy sequences Willis played the fetus.)

The detecting mixed with breakneck-speed dialogue and screwball comedy receded ever farther into the background... and the bottom dropped out of the ratings. When the series finally tried to return to wacky form near the end of its run, it seemed desperate and it was too late. Take, for example, "Plastic Fantastic Lovers," an episode written by Jerry Stahl, who went on to write

Permanent Midnight, a memoir about his harrowing descent into heroin addiction during the period he was a story editor on the show. In the episode, the detectives' client is a *Phantom of the Opera*-like recluse who's been disfigured by a cold and manipulative plastic surgeon. To add insult to the injury the surgeon also is having an affair with the recluse's beautiful wife, as well as with his zaftig nurse (played breathily by Jennifer Tilly). By the end of the story, all the suspects have tried to kill the dastardly doctor, but it turns out the butler did it. There's the obligatory battle in the surgeon's office, with the butler hurling rubber noses from a display case (one is labeled "Mark Harmon"; several others, "Michael Jackson"). In the finale the bad guy arms himself with a liposuction machine, while David wields a prosthetic limb to subdue him. By the end of the 1988–89 season, the show was history, its final episode watched by a mere ten percent of the audience.

(Incidentally, Mark Harmon, who played Maddie's astronaut lover, made a bit of network history a decade later, in the autumn of 1999, when he delivered the line "shit happens" on an episode of CBS's *Chicago Hope*. It was almost certainly the first time an actor in a prime-time series had uttered that particular epithet. It was a line that might be applied as well to *Moonlighting's* self-destructive demise.)

IN TV-LAND, CONVENTIONAL WISDOM PROCLAIMING THE "DEATH" of a particular genre only applies until that genre's next big hit. So it was for the half-hour situation comedy, which had fallen out of favor some time before.

When it premiered, *The Cosby Show* was a modest sitcom for which NBC's fondest hope was that it would manage a decent second place in its time period. But then, *Cosby* knocked off mighty *Magnum, P.I.*, a one-hour series that owed no small part of its success to the picturesque Hawaiian background (i.e., pretty girls in bikinis) and to its laid-back, beefcake-P.I. hero (Tom Selleck, a former model), perpetually attired in colorful Hawaiian shirts and baggy shorts. The race was on to fill prime time with half-hour sitcoms again.

LONG-RUNNING SERIES BECOME INSTITUTIONS, AND THAT'S PARticularly true of the one set in the Boston bar "where everybody knows your name."

Characters came and went. The bar changed hands (and then changed back again). Ultimately, the expert ensemble comedy of *Cheers* (1982–1993) turned on the grudging personal progress of one man, Sam "Mayday" Malone (Ted Danson), former big-league pitcher and recovering alcoholic, who began by caring about just two things—his hair and nailing babes—and ended as a sensitive nineties guy, working through his personal "issues."

Sam and Diane Chambers (Shelley Long) were opposites who attracted, but were horrified by it. They bickered, dated, had sex. Eventually they broke up.

Shelley Long left and the show went on, at the top of the ratings for another half decade, with Kirstie Alley as Rebecca Howe. Sam and Rebecca also were opposites who attracted, and they bickered and eventually had sex, too.

After their first time, in the bar's back office, endearingly insecure Rebecca says ardently: "It was one of the most powerful things that's ever happened to me in my life."

To which Sam cavalierly replies: "You gotta get out more."

But even this is progress for chauvinist Sam, who for once can't bring himself to brag to his bar cronies about his latest conquest.

"He lives to talk about that stuff," says disbelieving Carla (Rhea Perlman), the bar's tiny but tough-talking and randy waitress.

"And we live to hear about it," adds barfly Norm (George Wendt).

Rebecca is touched by this gentlemanly consideration, but Sam, newly sensitive, waves her expression of thanks away.

"I've never had a friend before," he says simply.

"But you have *lots* of friends," she replies with feeling, trying to reassure him.

"No, no, I've never *had* a friend before," Sam says.

Perhaps one of the funniest, deadpan *Cheers* episodes, though, came near the end of the series' long run, with Sam finally at a Sexaholics Anonymous meeting, driven there after all his friends have agreed he's too obsessed with sex ever to be married and monogamous. Finally, he asks his ever-loyal barmaid if she'd marry him.

"You're a hound. I can't marry a hound," Carla says quite sensibly. "I just thought I'd be the woman you cheated on your wife with."

Ever-sexed Carla could be counted on reliably for racy, just-one-of-the-guys jokes. Upon meeting a handsome handyman (Tom Skerritt, who later played Sheriff Jimmy Brock on *Picket Fences*), for example, with his name written above his work shirt pocket, she offers to read anything else he might have on his body.

"I read Braille," she says brightly.

Fade-out, fade-in. Taking a tentative seat at the circle of Dr. Sutton's Sexual Compulsive Group, Sam tell them his name is . . . Steve.

"Hi, Steve," they all respond in unison.

Actually, that's not his name, Sam allows. "It's Bob."

"Hi, Bob," comes back the less than enthusiastic group response.

When he finally admits his name is Sam, he's greeted with dead silence, no supportive greeting, but he plunges in.

"When I was growing up it was a sign of manhood how many

women you shagged," Sam tells the group, insisting he's not shallow just because he loves sex—and his hair. But, okay, he finally admits, "I'm not that happy anymore," not satisfied any longer by all that "skirt-chasing."

This does get the group's approving applause and Sam basks in it. Then it's the turn of Rachel (Sharon Lawrence), a pretty, nicely put-together and very proper-seeming brunette, who's sitting next to him.

"The root of my behavior is my low self-esteem," she says primly. Growing up, she never thought she was pretty or that she had any particular talents. "The only time I felt special was when men were attracted to me sexually."

She recounts her downward spiral as a dispiriting progression, saying how she sleeps with anyone now on the first date and is controlled completely by her lust.

"It had to be dangerous," she whispers of her sexual encounters in alleyways, in elevators, in department store dressing rooms. "There is no limit to how low I will go!"

Obviously horrified by her own obsessive actions, but unburdening herself at last, she quickly adds: "No fantasy I won't fulfill."

The group fills the silence after she concludes with fervent, supportive applause, while Sam—that hound!—languidly stretches his arms, leaning in close to her.

"So," he says out of the corner of his mouth, "do you like Chinese food?"

BY THE LATE EIGHTIES, SITCOMS—FROM *FAMILY TIES* TO *PERFECT Strangers*, and from *Night Court* to *Cheers*—were all the rage once more. There was a new *Newhart* and a *New Leave It to Beaver,* and even a comedy about elderly ladies, *The Golden Girls,* the popular NBC sitcom wags dubbed "Miami Nice."

But the most innovative network sitcom of them all had to be ABC's *Roseanne*, which began its successful and influential nine-year run in 1988. *Roseanne* starred the crass and opinionated former stand-up comic with the braying laugh. It was the only network comedy about a struggling working-class, self-described "white trash" family, and it was the only situation comedy as ambitious, daring, and funny in its social criticism as *All in the Family* had once been.

The show's viewpoint—its star's viewpoint—was forthrightly feminist, and viewers might be forgiven for thinking that star and executive producer Roseanne, a sitcom diva of the first rank, was stating her own viewpoint succinctly in the episode in which youngest child D.J. (Michael Fishman) goes out on his first date with Lisa, an aggressive little girl who orders him around.

"Boys bullying girls is a step backwards," Roseanne Conner explains to her husband, Dan (John Goodman), "but girls bullying boys, that's the future."

Of course, the show was more sophisticated than Roseanne, either the star or the character, generally let on, so when D.J. gets into trouble because of the little girl, Dan ripostes, "A man helping a woman out, that's a step backwards. But you cleaning up your own mess, that's the future."

The lesson of the episode, the lesson D.J.—a boy, his mom says, who has modeled himself after Eddie Munster—was supposed to learn, is that men and women (that is, Dan and Roseanne) are equal.

Fair enough. The show anchored its Lanford, Illinois, working-class family in hardscrabble economic reality and regularly mocked the happy family conventions of the 1950s, as well as the sleek, upper middle-class strivers who populated the rest of prime time. Dan and Roseanne Conner were overweight, which did not mean they refrained from sex—quite the contrary. And from time to time, as when they took a room at the Blue Swan Motel on the twentieth anniversary of their "first time," they were shown in bed, their shoulders and perhaps their legs bare.

One episode, skewering expectations, had the men around the kitchen table, discussing their "feelings" and trying to be sensitive guys, while the women, sprawling on the living room couch, drank beers and smoked cigars.

"I had to hear it again last night from Dan," Roseanne mock complains. "I don't cuddle enough."

Says Jackie (Laurie Metcalf), her younger sister, puffing away: "I work hard all day. I come home, I want my dinner, a little zippety-do-dah. Slap him on the ass, I'm out like a light."

Replies Roseanne: "I always take a coupla extra minutes with Dan, y'know, to finish him off. Otherwise, I have t'lay there an' listen to him gripe."

The episode ends with Dan running from the kitchen in tears.

In another episode, early in the series' run, Dan begins skipping their usual Wednesday night lovemaking. Is he "wednesdaying" somebody else? Roseanne asks, but it turns out he's only dreaming about a hardware store clerk, who turns out to look and act a lot like Roseanne.

"In the dream," says Dan, "she treats me like I'm some kinda irresistible sex toy," and he whispers to Roseanne what he and his dream girl do in his reverie.

Replies Roseanne: "Dream on," but later she takes him into an elevator at the mall. "Hurry up," she commands as the door closes.

Roseanne also explored the sexual awakening and misadventures of the Conner daughters. In one Darlene (Sara Gilbert) confides to her sister that she was "felt up" by her boyfriend. In another episode Roseanne urges "protection" for Darlene, only to learn her daughter hasn't gone all the way yet. By the time Darlene is a freshman in college, though, she admits to having smoked pot, tried speed, and dropped acid "a couple times"—not exactly Wally and the Beav.

In 1994, Roseanne threatened to withhold an episode from ABC if it did not air with its much touted and analyzed "lesbian kiss." Of course, the episode aired. (The following year saw *Serving in Silence: The Margarethe Cammermeyer Story*, an impeccable, prestigious TV movie about the real-life career military officer who came out as a lesbian. The movie was produced by Barbra Streisand and Glenn Close, and Close starred. Perhaps only their joint clout could have had it made, with the depictions of "intimacy" between Margarethe and her lover Diane remaining intact. *Serving in Silence* won a 1995 Emmy for Outstanding Movie Made for Television. Streisand, this time with Whoopi Goldberg, is returning as executive producer of another lesbian-themed TV movie, which the Lifetime cable network has scheduled for 2001. *What Makes a Family* will be based on the true story of a lesbian who fought her late partner's parents in court for custody of their child.)

While the "lesbian kiss" was debated endlessly in the press, *Roseanne* regularly set new (and hilarious) standards of candor through the character of officious Leon Carp (Martin Mull), who, as the saying goes, just happened to be gay. One episode, also late in the series' run, set in the diner, is all about "doing it" in inappropriate places. A sexy blonde waitress, mooning around because her boyfriend broke up with her, can't bring herself to clean off a particular table.

"Why not?" Jackie, Roseanne's long-suffering sister, wants to know.

Because it was *their* table.

"But you never ate dinner there," Jackie says, gasping in shock when she realizes exactly what the waitress means.

Later, the moony blonde says she won't clean out the ice machine either. After much banter about doing it in cars and outdoors, Jackie drags her husband into the darkened diner after hours, so they can do it on the table, too. But he's squeamish. He doesn't want to do it on the table because it's too rickety or on the counter because it's not clean enough, even though he does agree that "sex is supposed to be dirty." Finally, reluctantly, Jackie takes him home.

In the darkened diner a tall, thin figure who's hiding behind the counter stands. "I thought they'd never leave, baby," he says.

In his black muscle shirt and with his mop of wavy black hair, he must be the waitress's boyfriend. But then . . . . Leon rises beside him. "Should *we* go do it on the table?" Muscle Shirt asks.

"Let's try the ice machine," Leon replies.

In another episode (written, incidentally, by *Roseanne's* supervising producer, Chuck Lorre, the creator of *Dharma & Greg*), D.J. keeps peeking in on Becky, Roseanne's older daughter, when she's naked in the bathroom.

"Now he'll grow up gay for sure," says Darlene, the waspish younger daughter.

Later on, after Roseanne makes him promise to stop peeking at Becky, D.J. switches over to peeking in at Darlene.

Roseanne dealt remarkably candidly with teen and even preteen sexuality. In fact, the punchline to the episode in which D.J. goes out with the bullying little girl turns out not to have anything to do with equality and learning to stand up for yourself; instead, D.J. turns out to like assertive little Lisa because she "slipped" him "the tongue."

"D.J.'s finally got a friend that's not imaginary," Darlene says gleefully in still another episode, reporting to her parents that their youngest child is masturbating in the bathroom upstairs.

And in another episode, the thirteen-year-old D.J. is going through puberty, suffering through the embarrassment of spontaneous erections in the classroom. Roseanne, to reassure him, tells the story of her own puberty embarrassment, about how her mother bought a beautiful white dress for the junior-high prom, and that when she put it on and looked down, there was a stain. D.J., of course, doesn't understand. So Roseanne explains patiently that it was because she was having her first period. D.J. runs screaming from the room.

Roseanne, a lightning rod for criticism and controversy, even mocked network censorship in a brief snippet over the end credits of the D.J.'s erections episode. She's sitting at the table, on the kitchen set talking to the "network censor," who tells her none of "these expressions" are suitable.

"What about 'pitching the trouser tent'?" asks Roseanne. "Bootin' up the hard drive? Charming the anaconda? Raising the draw bridge, popping a wheelie, standing up for democracy? Waving to your chin?"

"No," says the censor each time. "No. There's absolutely, positively no way these are going to get on the air!"

Roseanne looks at the camera and smiles beatifically.

The censor turns. "Izzat on?" he asks querulously.

The camera nods up and down.

"Aw, shit," he says, the epithet no less obvious for being electronically masked.

ON THE NATIONAL POLITICAL SCENE THE SAME YEAR *ROSEANNE* premiered, TV evangelist Pat Robertson, head of the Christian Broadcasting Network, came in second in the New Hampshire

Republican presidential primary, demonstrating the power of the organized Christian Conservative Right, while accusations of marital infidelity drove Democratic Senator Gary Hart, that year's liberal hope, right out of the race. And a few print and TV journalists worried openly that some civilized border had been crossed, leading to who knew what in the unknown territory where the tabloids and the paparazzi lurked, even as every one of their reports included *that* photograph—the tousled Colorado Senator vacationing on the yacht named *Monkey Business*, a young woman (not his wife) perched prettily on his lap.

That year, the Christian Right, espousing traditionalism and "family values," which often included strong anti-gay, anti-feminist, anti-abortion beliefs, was widely believed to be *the* powerful new force in electoral politics. And the traditional broadcast networks were beset by very well-organized campaigns against both sex and violence in their programming (but particularly the former).

When NBC proposed to air *Roe* v. *Wade*, a 1989 television movie starring Holly Hunter as the woman whose Supreme Court victory established the right to legal abortions, twenty-three of the movie's original twenty-four sponsors withdrew in the face of boycotts threatened by anti-abortion groups. To the network's credit, and despite its obvious unease at being targeted, the movie aired.

Beginning in the late eighties, the Big Three networks, already buffeted by change and beset by old critics and bold new competitors, also had to contend with yet another national broadcast entity, competing directly for viewers and advertising dollars: Fox Broadcasting, the long-predicted Fourth Network.

Fox, the network, was created out of media assets (a major Hollywood film and TV studio, Twentieth Century Fox, and a major-market station group, formerly known as Metromedia) owned by

the News Corporation, an international conglomerate. Its newspapers—in particular, the *National Star*, the *New York Post*, and the *Sun*
in London—were best known perhaps for a brazen tabloid style that
included cheesecake photos of pretty, sometimes bare-breasted, girls.

The new network had a clear demographic mandate, and advertisers liked the sound of it: Go younger, go hipper! That trans-
lated into such witty innovations as *In Living Color*, which brought
hip-hop humor and the Fly Girls, a rubber-faced comic billed as
James Carrey, and the limp-wristed "The Men On..." sketches
that so upset gay activists, to prime time. Fox also aired *The Tracey
Ullman Show* and, spun off from it, *The Simpsons,* as well as such
boom-bada-boom sitcoms as *Martin* and *Married... With Children.*

LOVE AND MARRIAGE, LOVE AND MARRIAGE, GO TOGETHER LIKE
a—well, like Al and Peg Bundy and a vibrator joke.

Married... With Children was originally developed with the
hopes that Roseanne and the late Sam Kinnison would star. It aspired to be *All in the Family,* but with the Lear touch—controversial social issues of the day played for laughs—replaced by
leering, flatulence jokes, and the like. Both Archie Bunker and Al
Bundy (Ed O'Neill) cared passionately about the commode, but
only Archie was exercised about the Commies and only Peg
(Katey Sagal) had a collection of vibrators (Edith wouldn't have
known what one was).

Married (1987–1997) was reminiscent of the shtick Garry Marshall sitcoms of the mid-seventies, too; the Bundys were like the
Cunninghams (and even Laverne and Shirley), only anatomically
correct. *Married* may have been crass and juvenile, with one of the
most irritating laugh tracks since the earliest days of TV, but its
very shamelessness got laughs.

And despite, perhaps because of, being the target of outraged protests (for an episode showing a woman with her back to the camera taking off her bra and a man wearing a garter belt, and for its general "anti-family" views, among other things), it became the new network's most popular series.

For a modest little sitcom, a show its creators billed as "not the Cosbys," *Married* was immensely influential, both for Fox, which aired it, and for the other broadcast networks. And not only because it extended the reach of what was permissible for over-the-air TV, but because its no-taste humor was genuinely funny, and therefore held a mirror up to the viewers, posing the vexing question, "If this is in such poor taste, then why am *I* laughing?"

When a market research expert told the *Married* creators that his testing showed that the Bundy family needed to be made more lovable and caring, one of the producers famously replied, "You're the reason why television sucks."

In just one episode we learn that Al keeps porn magazines under the couch pillow and that the henpecked neighbor is expected to provide his wife with her daily "nooner." Later, on a trip to London, the same neighbors, thinking they're at the theater, wind up at the Red Fanny, an S&M club, dressed in enough leather to do Emma Peel proud.

It's not just the Bundy elders who are obsessed with sex. "I too can be strummed and twanged," Kelly (Christina Applegate), their sexpot daughter, plaintively tells her Old World date, who's singing romantically (if obliviously) to her while playing his guitar.

In another episode (which the network decided at the time it was prudent not to air), to spice up their nonexistent love life Al and Peg go to a motel, recommended to them by their friends Steve and Marcy, that has X-rated videos available. The tape they get, though, they realize, is of Steve and Marcy having sex—and they've been taped having sex as well! Both couples sue. The jury awards Steve and Marcy ten thousand dollars, but the Bundys get nothing because the "act was so short the jury couldn't determine if sex had taken place." In other episodes that raised (or lowered) the bar of what was acceptable:

- While on a camping trip, three women start their menstrual periods simultaneously. At the network's request, the episode was retitled from "A Period Piece" to "The Camping Show."

- Another time, Al, Peg, and neighbor Marcy (Amanda Bearse) have a conversation about breasts.

  Says Marcy: "You know what would happen if men had breasts?" Al: "We wouldn't need women anymore?"

  To which Peg replies: "And if you had what other men have, I wouldn't need batteries."

  To which Al ripostes: "So *that's* what happened to my Die-Hard."

- In yet another episode, Al's "remote-control override" overrides not only Peg's TV channel picks, but all her electronic "devices," including "Big Otis." While watching Peg on the couch watching *Oprah*, we hear a commercial come on for "Earthpads," the "only feminine hygiene product recycled from yesterday's garbage."

  Later, Peg and Al's slutty daughter, wearing black spandex shorts and a sports bra, comes in from an aerobics class across town. She had to take the bus back, Kelly says obliviously, and every man on the bus offered her a seat, but nobody would get up to give it to her. Not only that, she adds, indignant, but a "turban-clad gentleman" she calls the "man of a thousand boils" told her that if she rubbed his "magic lamp" a genie would "come out."

Pausing a beat, she announces to a hysterical laugh track: "There was no genie."

All this was certain to draw the ire of both the professional "family values" protesters—not only the Reverend Donald Wildmon, who by then headed both Christian Leaders for Responsible Television and the American Family Association—but "average citizen" Terry Rakolta, a Midwestern housewife and mother of four, whose letter of complaint to a major *Married* sponsor, Coca-Cola, resulted in its withdrawal from the show and, not incidentally, a barrage of publicity for herself.

Although the show was mostly just low humor and cheap laughs, occasionally the producers did strike back at their critics. For example, in the episode in which Al makes a movie called *A Day in the Life of a Shoe Salesman*, using his ten-thousand-dollar government grant to hire bikini-clad models to be the "customers." In addition to a zinger about the Republicans and wife-swapping, and a reference to Supreme Court Justice Clarence Thomas and pornography, the episode's punchline was this: The National Education Association, a frequent target of Senator Jesse Helms and others for its grants to "pornography" in the real world, is disbanded in the episode for funding Al Bundy's movie.

Are you laughing yet? How about now: When a woman is finally attracted to Al, with an almost surreal appropriateness she's played by *Wheel of Fortune's* Vanna White.

THE BUNDYS MAY HAVE ASPIRED TO BE THE BUNKERS, THOUGH more animated and with a hipper twist, but that honor actually fell to another Fox innovation—the return of the prime-time animated half-hour show.

It's easy to forget how few animation series that adults could watch were ever on TV before *The Simpsons* (1989 to present) came along. There was *Rocky and Bullwinkle* in the late fifties, of course, a witty series, but it was never, ever risqué.

Homer J. Simpson (the "J" in his name, by the way, is an homage to Jay Ward, *Rocky and Bullwinkle's* creator) and his blue-haired wife, Marge, on the other hand, even get caught naked in public in one episode. In another episode, Homer is powerfully tempted by a cute coworker at the nuclear plant, who shares his taste for donuts (and was "voiced" by actress Michelle Pfeiffer).

Typical of *The Simpsons'* casual sophistication about bawdy matters is the episode in which ten-year-old Bart discovers that the "witch" next door runs a burlesque house that's a Springfield tradition. It's a "house of ill fame, a house of loose ethics," says Marge, sharing her "moral outrage" at a town meeting, chaired by the town's lascivious mayor, who turns out to be a patron. Others patronizing the house include Bart's grandfather, the Cagneyesque but clueless chief of police, and the school principal. "I was only there to get directions to get away from there," Principal Skinner claims.

"Lady, I gotta tell yah, I been grossly misinformed about witches," Bart says, getting his first glimpse of the garter-belt-flashing can-can girls dancing inside.

"We put the spring in Springfield," the can-can girls sing.

Homer and his father put the spring in Springfield, too, in a 1994 episode that prefigured the Viagra craze, by taking to the road with a medicine show, selling a "revitalization tonic."

After eleven years of marriage, Marge is distressed because the "Homie fires" are flickering out. Instead of making love to her, Homer would rather watch *Uncle Dooby and the Great Frisco Freakout*, starring (but of course) Troy McClure (one of the many unctuous voices the late Phil Hartman contributed to the show) for the tenth time on TV—even though she's wearing a thigh-length diaphanous purple nightgown with an, ahem, plunging neckline.

There's too much pressure, Homer moans, so he and Marge address their marital difficulties by heading off, kids in tow, to the local mall bookstore for a self-help book. But they don't want the little ones to know they're perusing the *Kama Sutra*. So when Lisa (enthusing over the latest tome by Al Gore) and Bart (holding up a UFO conspiracy tract) run up, Marge and Homer grab the first books at hand—*Tanks of the Third Reich* for her, a Robert Mapplethorpe picture book for him.

Yikes!

Home at last with their covert purchase—(a guidebook on tape by conservative radio commentator Paul Harvey for "Mr. and Mrs. Erotic American")—they set about following its staccato-voiced suggestions: First a bath together... (They get stuck.)

Then a romantic getaway... (To the Aphrodite Inn, where the only "theme" room left is the Utility Room, where, rather dubiously, Homer suggests they can play the janitor and his wife.)

But nothing works, which is where Abe Simpson, Homer's querulous old dad and a reluctant resident of the Springfield Retirement Castle, animatedly enters the picture with a "home remedy that will put the dowsers back in your trousers." Homer knocks back a few gulps and runs home to Marge, who, later, dreamily pronounces him to be "Rex Harrison and Paul Anka rolled into one."

And so begins another Homer Simpson scheme—to sell the revitalizing elixir to needy towns like Mount Seldom, Frigid Falls, and Lake Flaccid. But when all the men of Springfield start imbibing Simpson & Son's Liquid Lothario, lovemaking runs rampant.

And the children, stirred up by Bart who's been studying his

UFO book, decide their parents are going to bed early as part of a fiendish plot to eliminate dinner.

ARGUABLY, FOX BROADCASTING'S BIGGEST, MOST CONTROVERSIAL innovation in the late eighties, however, arose directly from the parent corporation's tabloid experience, and that innovation went by the telling press moniker of "Trash TV."

A Current Affair and *America's Most Wanted*, both on Fox, and *Geraldo* and company, in syndication, specialized in titillation and true crime. Their perfect subject was the lurid sex crime, and they vied to bring into American living rooms soundbites from actual sleazoid participants, mixed with dubious "recreations" of tabloid headline stories, including the Preppie Murder Case, the Night Stalker, and the Long Island Lolita.

(The case of teenaged Amy Fisher, the so-called Long Island Lolita, who tried to murder her older, married lover's wife, resulted in not one but *three* TV movies—one on each of the three broadcast networks. The three Amys were Noelle Parker on NBC, Alyssa Milano on CBS, and Drew Barrymore on ABC.)

The shows all garnered high ratings and wholesale imitators, and in the rush to add entertainment and human interest "value," the carefully nurtured reputation of television news, both on the local and on the Big Three network level, was tarnished and diminished, seemingly overnight.

The success of tabloid TV increased the pressure for sensationalism in network prime time, too. While Geraldo Rivera, to many the personification of the new, anything-goes TV journalism, was doing stories about prostitution and sexual abuse on his syndicated show, and having his nose broken in an unscripted brawl on the set, NBC, by then the number one network, was airing *Favorite Son*, a miniseries that broke new thematic ground with its graphic depiction of sexual bondage, as well as a critically reviled, but highly rated special about satanism, hosted by none other than Geraldo Rivera.

Favorite Son (1988), based on a popular novel of the same name (by former NBC marketing and promotion executive Steve Sohmer, who coined the memorable "Same Time, Better Network" line for one campaign), aspired to be the *Manchurian Candidate* of its time, and it spun off a short-lived series. But, of course, it was most memorable for one particular thing, and that was the bondage scene.

In it, a senator's female press aide strips down to bra, panties, garters, and stockings and asks an FBI agent to tie her to the bedpost. Characters had been cuffed and tied since the earliest days of TV—it even happened to Lucy and Ricky—and of course it was always played for vaudeville style, bada-boom laughs. But this was the first time it was played so explicitly and, as it were, straight— as kinky pleasure—in network prime time. The producer defended the scene, calling it "character driven."

Favorite Son was one token of the old networks' new direction in the face of the tough new competition. There were others. For instance, an NBC TV movie called *The Sex Tapes* was a detective story set in the world of S&M brothels. It starred (for extra promotional juice) Vanessa Williams, the former Miss America who had been stripped of her tiara for having posed nude in lesbian photos. The movie offered background glimpses of leather whips and manacles, and a dominatrix in a black corset and fishnet stockings.

Elsewhere on the Peacock Network, brief glimpses of bare (male) bottoms spiced up episodes of both *L.A. Law* and *St. Elsewhere*. One *L.A. Law* episode, with scenes in a nudist colony, showed a naked woman from the back, albeit with the shot cropped at about what would have been her bikini line.

On one episode of NBC's long-running *Cheers*, Sam Malone felt like a *putz*, a Yiddish word that means both "penis" and, roughly, "worthless idiot," because he had an embarrassing erection in a restaurant.

On an episode of ABC's *thirtysomething*, Hope and Michael were shown in bed together, under the sheets and obviously having sex, and *discussing* his putz—namely, whether or not he should "pull out" before reaching orgasm.

Over on CBS, in an episode of *Murphy Brown*, the sitcom set in a *60 Minutes*-style news magazine, a character actually uttered the word "putz," setting off alarms about the perceived decline of the Tiffany Network.

But the most telling indicator of what might now be acceptable on the airwaves was this: Where once an individual censor might have reviewed every episode of every Big Three network prime-time show, by the end of the 1980s, two of the Big Three (NBC and CBS) had closed down almost entirely their Standards and Practices departments, as the censors were known. At ABC, too, the S&P staff was drastically cut back. Whatever the professed reason (cost savings, network spokesmen sniffed), the effect was to remove any internal counterweight to the already heavy pressure for racier, more cutting-edge programming.

That lasted only a few years. By the mid-nineties even Fox, the network that, as part of its initial hoopla, had billed itself as the only one that was entirely censor-free, had a functioning, albeit more relaxed, Department of Standards and Practices.

"Live from New York, It's . . . ." Once it was fashionable to dismiss *Saturday Night Live*, the warhorse of late night comedy, which debuted in 1975. In fact, when the show's original "not ready for prime time" players moved on to the movies,

NBC nearly cancelled it. But *SNL* kept coming back, reinvigorating itself with fresh cast members and confounding its critics, who tend to forget that the key word in the show's name is LIVE.

Among the comedians and comic actors who took their turns in the *SNL* ensemble (or became closely associated with it) are Dan Aykroyd, John Belushi, Dana Carvey, Chevy Chase, Billy Crystal, Jane Curtin, Robert Downey Jr., Julia Louis-Dreyfus, Chris Farley, Al Franken, Janeane Garofalo, Christopher Guest, Phil Hartman, Jan Hooks, Jon Lovitz, Norm Macdonald, Steve Martin, Dennis Miller, Eddie Murphy, Bill Murray, Mike Myers, Joe Piscopo, Gilda Radner, Chris Rock, Adam Sandler, Martin Short, and David Spade.

And like the live shows of the early days, because it airs live—at least on the East Coast—anything can, and just might, happen, such as the moment in 1981 when Charles Rocket uttered the word "fuck" on one live broadcast. Or the notorious late-eighties penis sketch: To demonstrate that the grip of censorship had been loosened at the networks, the cast, ostensibly naked behind a bar in a nudist club, repeated the word "penis" in nearly every sentence. Or that time Sinead O'Connor tore up the photo of the Pope.

SNL, though not ready for prime time, has been in its first quarter-century a mighty engine pushing at the boundaries of American television—the "most pervasive influence on the art of comedy in contemporary culture," as the *New York Times* called it on the occasion of its twenty-fifth anniversary.

And it's still doing it with a cast that includes Jimmy Fallon, Will Ferrell, Ana Gasteyer, Darrell Hammond, Chris Kattan, Tim Meadows, Cheri Oteri, Colin Quinn, and Molly Shannon, and skits such as the dead-on parody in which a belligerently dim-witted Sean Connery, a contestant on *Celebrity Jeopardy*, misreads the pen-is-mightier category as "The Penis Mightier."

Or this topical satire, which aired in the late nineties, at the very height of the Clinton impeachment imbroglio: An expert panel on oral sex has been convened to appear before the House Judiciary Committee. As the camera pans slowly down the panel, we see that on it are such worthies as Courtney Love, Mariah Carey, Elizabeth Dole, Richard Simmons, and George Michael.

Now that's funny.

The Nineties

Jerry to Tony and Cicely to South Park

"YOU SUCK!" A LITTLE GIRL ON *UNCLE BUCK*, A SHORT-LIVED CBS "family hour" sitcom, said to her brother, igniting the decade's first great battle over morality and declining standards on network TV. But worse, the moralizing majoritarians feared, was shortly to come.

In one year in the early nineties, according to anti-smut crusader Reverend Wildmon's American Family Association, the three networks together broadcast more than ten thousand sexual "incidents" during prime time, with fourteen scenes depicting sex outside of the sacred bonds for every single act of sexual intercourse between married people.[31]

Around the same time another, and arguably more objective, survey of sex on TV found that by 1989 not only did married couples *not* have sex on TV, but they didn't even talk about it. That survey, by a Florida State University professor, compared one 1989 week of prime-time network programming with that same week a decade before, in 1979.

The survey found that sex talk was up (sixteen instances in

1989 versus thirteen in 1979) and explicit sex acts were up (four versus none), while sexual equality seemed on the wane (men initiated two thirds of the sexual behavior and three-quarters of the sex acts in 1989 versus a rough parity a decade before). Most significantly, in that 1989 prime-time week there was not one single mention of AIDS.[32]

About this time, the FCC weighed in with its own definition of "indecent" programming; namely, that which was "patently offensive" to "prevailing" community standards. But in the deregulated spirit of the times, and over the strong objections of the socially conservative and Religious Right protesters, the FCC mandated in 1987 that even indecent programming was permissible—between the hours of midnight and six A.M., when the children presumably were tucked safely in bed. By 1990, however, the FCC had expanded that window for "indecency" to be from eight P.M. to six A.M.

1990 was the year David Lynch's *Twin Peaks* (1990–1991) came to network television. Moody and suggestive—as well as flawed and short-lived, but hugely hyped—this attempt by the director of *Blue Velvet* to bring his sense of all-American surrealism to network television turned on murder and incest, and included both a small-town brothel and teen hookers.

Before it collapsed in obscurantism and mystery dwarves, though, *Peaks* made a teen nymphet's trick of tying a knot in a cherry stem with her tongue into a promise of expertly kinky oral sex.

1990 WAS ALSO THE YEAR *SEINFELD* (1990–1998) PREMIERED, TO what at first were only modest ratings. The show about nothing, which turned into *the* ratings juggernaut of nineties network television, was actually about one thing, and that thing was invariably S-E-X. The myriad examples of yada-yada...well, you be the judge:

- Jerry boffing the maid

- The deaf woman who can't tell the difference between "sex" and "six" and incorrectly lip-reads "sweeping together" as "sleeping together"?

- The girlfriend whose name Jerry can't remember, but knows it rhymes with a female body part, so he guesses Mulva, but her name turns out to be Dolores

- Elaine's Christmas card photograph of herself, which Kramer took, in which one nipple is showing

- George suddenly getting alarmingly smarter after he stops having sex because his girlfriend has mono. But when Elaine stops so her boyfriend can concentrate on passing his exams to become a doctor, it has the opposite effect, and he dumps her

- The is it or isn't it low-fat yoghurt episode, in which Jerry accidentally swears in front of a neighbor kid, who promptly imitates him (the expletives were bleeped out)

- The backwards episode about tall, blonde, braless Sue Ellen's wedding in India that's derailed when Elaine admits she slept with the groom (who's named "Pinter," in a homage to *Betrayal*, the 1983 film about a love triangle, written by Harold Pinter, that also tells its narrative by stepping backward through time)

- The one about the bet to see who can keep from doing *that* the longest

- Or the one about the gassy horse, the marble rye, and the sax player who blows his audition because he's just performed cunnilingus on Elaine.

And in what might have been another episode but was so-called real life, a man in the workplace who repeated the plot of a *Seinfeld* episode to a female coworker was subsequently the subject of a sexual harassment suit.

Then there was the one about the hooker parking lot and Kramer's Technicolor dream coat, in which Jerry takes offense when both a clothing store salesman and a girl selling flowers in a restaurant assume he's not "with" Elaine. That umbrage continues later when Jerry finds himself at an outdoor restaurant, sipping champagne with Ethan, the carrot-headed, plainly gay wig master for the touring company of *Joseph and the Technicolor Dream Coat*, who's staying with George and his fiancée Susan.

Another young gay man, Jesse, who introduces himself as George Hamilton's personal assistant, turns up and invites Ethan out on a date. "How do you know *we're* not together?" Jerry says irately. "It's very emasculating," he huffs in an aside.

That's George's feeling, too, when he discovers a condom in his car and learns that Jiffy Park, the bargain lot on Twelfth Avenue, lets streetwalkers use the parked autos for their whorehouse.

"What do you people call it," he sputters to a bosomy honey-blonde in a short skirt and a tight spandex top with—what else?—a plunging neckline, "turning tricks?" And that's the point at which his fiancée turns up.

Of course, Kramer, who's been given a loaner pink Cadillac Eldorado by the lot's manager, ends up wearing the Technicolor dream coat and a floppy felt hat that the wind has blown his way. Carrying an ornate walking stick that he got from Elaine and bopping along to a rap beat, he's the perfect picture of a pimp, and when he gets to the hooker parking lot and pulls the honey-blonde whore out of his car and begins struggling with her, the cops arrive. The episode ends on a freeze frame of shocked, disheveled Kramer and the hooker in mid-fight.

Appropriately enough, the series ended its long run with its self-absorbed foursome in jail, convicted of violating a good samaritan law for merely watching (and quipping) while a robbery took place. By then, though, *Seinfeld* had spawned a whole prime-time schedule of imitators about neurotic urban singles and their obsession with sex.

As one TV producer described the *Seinfeld* era's NBC Monday night line-up, which then included *Caroline in the City, Suddenly Susan,* and *The Naked Truth,* it was "pretty white chicks living in New York who can't get laid."[33]

As for the "decent" stuff on TV, sweet-natured shows like *Northern Exposure*, the surprise hit of the early nineties on CBS, weren't nearly decent enough for some. Senator Jesse Helms of North Carolina, for example, repeatedly introduced or supported legislation to outlaw "indecency" and to further circumscribe the "sleaze" and "explicit" sexuality "flooding" the airwaves. In the mid-eighties he had terrified the Tiffany Network by proposing to raise enough money from his supporters to buy CBS, a ploy that in retrospect seems more like a publicity stunt than a real possibility. And in an influential 1992 speech, Dan Quayle, then the Vice President of the United States, lambasted fictional TV newswoman *Murphy Brown* for a story that had her bearing a child "out of wedlock." Ironically, when another fictional single professional woman on TV had done the same thing the year before, on *The Days and Nights of Molly Dodd*, the blessed event passed without much notice.

Of course, 1992 was a presidential election year, and Vice President Quayle's anti-Hollywood speech was one proven way to enlist the organized forces of the Moral Majority and the Christian Right in the Republicans' fight. That was the year that 17 percent of actual voters were white Christians who identified themselves with the religious right, according to exit polls, and nearly two-thirds of those voters cast ballots for the Republican presidential candidate. But that was the year of "It's the economy, stupid," and the battle was won with a Boomer, widely regarded as both a master politician and something of a womanizer, in the White House.

FOR THOSE WHO PREFERRED THEIR TV SEX SANCTIFIED BY THE bonds of matrimony, there should have been some consolation in the popularity of *Mad About You* (1992–1999). After all, outraged social conservatives had been pointing with alarm at surveys showing that while sex on TV was increasing exponentially, sex between *married people* on television was practically nonexistent.

The half-hour sitcom, starring Paul Reiser and Helen Hunt as Paul and Jamie Stemple Buchman, was the show that most definitely brought the oomph back into matrimony. Sex within marriage was, in the words of the show's song, the "final frontier" that newlyweds Paul and Jamie were heading into.

The premiere episode, which was set a few months after their marriage, ended with Paul and Jamie, who hadn't had sex in five days, finally, in desperation, doing it on the kitchen counter while their party guests milled about in the living room. That display of impropriety miffed the conservative critics, who didn't seem at all mollified that, at least, Paul and Jamie were hitched.

Critics from the left, meanwhile, took offense later in the

show's run when the heat between the couple, no longer newly-weds but harried parents, preoccupied with jobs, housekeeping and raising a child, was so obviously turned down.

And then there was the episode in which Paul and Jamie set aside an evening to try to have sex. "No talking about mothers in the bedroom," Paul proclaims. And they keep getting inter-rupted—by her mom on the phone, by their dog Murray bound-ing repeatedly across the bed on a never-ending hunt for an imaginary mouse, by thoughts of filmmaking and the obligations of the day, and even by the need to pee.

"You know I can't do it with him here," Jamie says, noticing the dog at the foot of the bed staring up at them as they neck. Finally, they decide to just do it.

"Just like that, bing bang boom?" Paul asks incredulously.

"At this point I'd settle for the boom," says Jamie.

And Paul begins to riff about how men just invented the bing and the bang to get to the boom.

One of the show's risqué high points arose from the simple (if rather prescient) premise that filmmaker Paul, commissioned by PBS to do a short documentary about his own life, has set up video cameras in every room of the apartment. Of course, when the cameras are on, he and Jamie don't act at all naturally.

Halfway through their stilted posturing, Jamie's feckless older sister Lisa (Anne Ramsay), wearing a long, buttoned-up coat over jeans, breezes in, ostensibly to return a video the couple has lent her. Oblivious to Paul's and Jamie's attempts to clue her in to the videotaping, she launches into a manic monologue about the meat packer "Daddy told me to stay away from" and Dennis, her married boyfriend.

"Dennis' wife is back in town," she announces, marching across the room, the gesticulating couple in her wake. "What am I sup-

posed to do, sit home alone? . . . It's not like he's so great or anything. I mean, how many times can you fake it?"

She stops and demonstrates for the camera she doesn't know is
there: "Dennis, oh Dennis," she moans. "Yeah, that's it. Right
there, baby! Yeah yeah! Oh my god, oh my god, you're the king!
Here I go . . . Ah-AH-AAH!"

Lisa starts up again, heading for the bedroom, declaiming all the
way about how the meat packer came over, then Dennis unexpectedly showed up and was so distraught she had to give him a
Percodan. Turning her back to the camera, and facing the couple,
Lisa opens her coat and lets it drop to the floor.

She's topless! Jamie's mouth drops open and Paul, pie-eyed,
torn between conflicting desires, twists pretzel-like, half covering
his eyes.

Nonchalantly, Lisa picks up a sweater and shrugs into it, talking
all the while, ignoring both Jamie's surprise and Paul's distress.
The meat packer has mob ties, she says, putting her coat back on.
She reverses field and heads back out. They went out for cannoli,
she adds, now she's meeting him for brunch.

Stopping in the open doorway, she sprays a breath freshener in
her mouth. "Wish me luck," she says, exiting.

As the door closes behind her, Paul and Jamie exchange a
look. He holds up the video. "Look, honey," he says brightly,
"*Roman Holiday.*"

But the episode that annoyed the conservative critics most came
late in the show's run, when Paul, sexually aroused by Viagra, fran-
tically searches Manhattan for his wife. The jokes were both about
Paul's desperation and his embarrassing erection, so when his
cousin suggested Paul should end his ordeal by relieving himself,
Paul shot back: "I ain't wasting this on a picture of Steffi Graf!"

The criticism from both ends of the spectrum not withstanding, the show ended its run on a high note with a sweet one-hour finale that shed a lot of warmth, and, because of Helen Hunt's sexy competence, no little heat, in the form of *Why I'm Like This*, a mock documentary by the Buchmans' grown-up daughter (played wittily by Janeane Garofalo) about her parents. The final episode flashes forward to when Paul gets a vasectomy and then to Paul and Jamie's separation and reconciliation in the year 2021.

AROUND THE SAME TIME AS A REAL VICE PRESIDENT OF THE United States made a fictional single newswoman's sex life a campaign issue, there was yet another telling indicator of what might now be acceptable, only this time what was intended to be a vivid and dramatic demonstration by a sophisticated TV executive for an exclusive, equally sophisticated audience went one bump and grind over the line.

During a senior management retreat at a Colorado ski resort, Fox Broadcasting's programming *wunderkind*, the thirtysomething Harvard-trained Stephen Chao, who'd just been appointed president of Fox TV, decided to prove that in America sex and nudity were more disturbing than graphic violence. As Chao spoke, outlining his thesis, a hired male dancer took the stage and did his act, stripping naked. The "senior managers" present for the provocative demonstration included not only Chao's big boss, Rupert Murdoch, but Richard Cheney, then the United States Secretary of Defense, and both of their wives.

How understanding was tabloid and media baron Murdoch about the vivid way Chao made his point? The *wunderkind* was fired that same June 1992 day. Perhaps he ran away to Alaska.

THE IMPRUDENT EXECUTIVE WOULD HAVE BEEN WELCOME IN charming Cicely, on the heretofore uncelebrated Alaskan Riviera, a haven for eccentrics where everyone appears to have been sprinkled with fairy dust.

In *Northern Exposure* (1990–1995), Dr. Joel Fleischman (Rob Morrow) is the classic fish out of water—a transplanted New Yorker who finds himself in Cicely working to pay off a medical loan. He and pixieish bush pilot Maggie O'Connell (Janine Turner) meet cute, as they must, annoy each other, and spar constantly.

On TV that means they're meant for each other, and eventually they're going to make love. And so, in due course, they do. But matters sexual and romantic (often with some bizarre medical twist that brings Dr. Joel in) are a concern of nearly epidemic proportions for all the residents of moonstruck Cicely (a town named, according to one of the show's producers, after the actress Cicely Tyson).

In one episode, "All Is Vanity," Dr. Joel and sixty-three-year-old Holling Vincoeur (John Cullum), the owner of the Brick, the local bar, discuss circumcisions. Holling wants to have one because he thinks it's "in style," and because his much younger "babe" girl-friend prefers "crewnecks" to "turtlenecks." Joel is opposed, both because it's unnecessary surgery and because "it" is a very sensitive part of the anatomy: "Stitches, Holling, stitches down *there*."

In another episode, Chris Stevens (John Corbett) finds himself in a monastery having disturbing, but irresistible sexual thoughts about another monk (who, of course, turns out to be a female, liv-ing secretly as a man).

And then there's Maggie, the spunky pilot from suburban Grosse Pointe, Michigan, so straight-arrow she flunks her own live-in boyfriend in his pilot's license renewal test when she finds out he's colorblind. (Later, he dies outrageously: struck by a falling satellite. This convinces Maggie that all her boyfriends are cursed—he was death number five—but that's another matter.)

In another post-boyfriend episode ("The Bumpy Road to Love," which introduces Adam and Eve, Cicely's unshaven, stringy-haired reclusive gourmet cook and his hypochondriacal wife, played by Adam Arkin and Valerie Mahaffey, who won an Emmy for the role), Maggie, knocking back shots at the Brick and getting rather toasted, is embittered by her bad luck with beaus, telling a less than fully comprehending Ed Chigliak (Darren E. Burrows), the town's male ingenue, that "men never really listen to you. . . . Oh, they pretend to listen. They nod and they grunt, but they don't really listen, you know?"

"Nope," says Ed, a long-haired Native American who aspires to be a filmmaker, just like his hero Woody Allen.

"It's the joystick," Maggie says. "Is it big enough? Where do they put it?" She throws back another shot. "Okay, sex is fine, sex is good." She smiles impishly. "Sex is *great*! Okay, we need men for sex. But do we need so many?" In the grand tradition of romantic comedy, Joel drives Maggie crazy, always on her nerves, always on her mind.

Isn't it obvious? Adam, the last frontier's grizzly barefoot gourmet chef and Cicely's all-around polymath, has the usual pithy explanation: "Just the thought of emotional intimacy turns you into an Eskimo Pie," he tells Maggie, who's affronted and jealous when Joel takes up briefly with Elaine, his former fiancée, visiting from New York.

And Fleischman? "Insecurity incarnate," Adam scoffs. "In the end he will be alone, miserable and very, very rich."

"And you, Maggie," he concludes, "will end up surrounded by cats."

In the series' charmingly twisted way, it's only after Elaine and Joel have the best sex they've ever had that they realize they're no longer in love.

But perhaps the most sensually-minded *Northern Exposure* episode of them all was "Only You," written by Ellen Herman. In it Chris Stevens becomes sexually irresistible to women.

"Hi, Chris," all the women of Cicely are crooning, smiling coquettishly up at him as he and Dr. Joel pass by. Chris matter-of-factly explains to the boggled Dr. Joel that it's just another instance of the Stevens family smell drawing women, that it happened to him before, and that it had happened to his father and paternal grandfather before him as well. A few men can smell the Stevens pheromones, too, he adds, and "it's a shock if they haven't come to terms with their feminine side."

Reminiscing about how he'd taken advantage of it himself in his younger days, Chris opines, "A roomful of naked eighteen-year-olds is great, but..."

Later, in his parked Airstream, surrounded by the panting ladies of Cicely, Chris tells Joel how the Stevens men have all done time, have all been juicers. Some have even married their cousins. Of course, Chris becomes obsessed with the only woman in town immune to his pheromones—those chemical messengers animals emit to attract the opposite sex—and she's Irene, the itinerant optometrist who travels the Alaskan outback in her Optomobile.

That night, mooning over Irene, Chris opines to Maurice (Barry Corbin), the ex-astronaut who's the little town's chief civic booster, that, "Thinkin' about a woman, doesn't know you're thinkin' about her, doesn't care, makes you think about her even more."

Cut to the next morning. Chris is glum, sitting outside the trailer. Out comes Patti, a pretty, long-haired brunette in a man's robe, followed by Linda, a little, short-haired blonde in a man's work shirt. They sit across from him, side by side, as he apologizes for his impotence.

"He couldn't focus," Patti tells Linda.

"You guys were great," Chris rushes to assure them. "Very giving, very sensitive. Very erotic."

"Thanks," they say in unison. "You, too."

Cut to Chris and Dr. Joel, who's puzzled to hear the Stevens Syndrome has gone away. "It's your body saying, 'I have my mate,'" he theorizes. "'I don't need another,'" even if that "mate" is Irene, who's uninterested.

Later on, Joel tells Maggie, who's obsessing once again about still being single while time is passing: "You're a knockout.... It's [just] your abrasive personality and the fact that you don't like us [men]."

Ruefully, Maggie accepts it as a compliment.

Meanwhile, on the radio, Chris is posing a pertinent philosophical question: "What are these elusive and ephemeral things that ignite passion in the human heart?"

The Optomobile rumbles out of town. Fade out.

Of course, in the real world beyond the city limits of little Cicely, Chris's question about igniting passion has significance, too. Apart from backwoods philosophers, perhaps the two population groups with the best, most heartfelt answers are teenagers and the advertisers who avidly sell to them.

DID AMERICANS FEAR THE YOUNG BEFORE THE ADVENT OF TELEVISION? Certainly, at least since Elvis Presley's televised pelvic "twitches" in the fifties, political leaders and concerned parents alike have pointed with alarm at the tube's deleterious influence on sneering youth (whether ducktailed, dreadlocked, or skinheaded), who listen to rock and roll, watch too much TV, and are said to be in the thrall of a two-headed demon named Sex and Violence.

By the early nineties, the worst kids—those who'd once been called "juvenile delinquents"—had long since traded in their easy-to-make zip guns for even easier-to-obtain Tech-9s. Not surprisingly, given that it was televised nightly on the local news and on "reality TV" shows, the belief grew widespread across the political spectrum that there was a youth violence crisis.

It wasn't just the kids by the middle of the decade either. With the likes of Mike Tyson's rape trial and O.J. Simpson's murder trial, the whole of the public discourse seemed at times to consist of the chanted mantra, "sex and violence, sex and violence."

"WHEEL'S ON FIRE ROLLING DOWN THE ROAD. NOTIFY MY NEXT of kin, this wheel shall explode . . . ."

If there was one single show gleefully leading the way when it came to *épater les bourgeois* and defying the prevailing values of political correctness, that show was most definitely not American.

Barbara Eden may have suffered through the great Navel Battle of *I Dream of Jeannie*, her belly button deemed too suggestive for the great American airwaves, but for those two trendy Londoners of *Absolutely Fabulous* (1992–1996), Edina and Patsy (Jennifer Saunders and Joanna Lumley), it was an entirely different story, sweetie.

Edina, also known as Eddie, at her wit's end while redecorating, decides to pop over to Manhattan via Concorde for an afternoon's shopping with Patsy, her fashion X-ray friend. They pull into a Lower East Side tattoo parlor so Eddie can get pierced for a navel ring. Later, we are treated not only to the sight of Eddie's pierced navel, but she makes perfectly certain that we can see how in the interim it's gotten red, swollen, and infected, as well.

"We're not the bloody Waltons, are we?" she blusters at Saffron (Julia Sawalha), her mortified, aching-for-comformity teenage daughter, who suffers such indignities as finding herself on the mailing list of the "Karl Lagerfeld Bondage Room at Club 64" in New York.

When Saffron discovers her mom and Patsy going through a porn magazine, she takes one quick glance at a photo spread and says, "That's so degrading to women."

"What do you mean?" Patsy sneers over her shoulder. "*She's* got the whip!"

Patsy and Eddie: Fabulous these two Brit twits might have been—their drug habits stuck in the sixties—but they were also among the most dysfunctional of all TV families, absolutely the most snide and cutting in episode after episode chockablock with hilarious throwaway barbs about sex, drugs, and fashionability. This was the basic, ever-so extended *Ab Fab* "family":

- Eddie, alternately plaintive and willful, crazed for acceptance by the fashionable and the hip, and for "LaCroix, sweetie, LaCroix"

- Patsy, her best (and only) pal, reed thin and promiscuous, both when it came to one-night stands and to ingesting massive quantities of drugs and alcohol. She prefers a "'champers, Eddie" or "a Stoli, babe," and only the most expensive cocaine. Perhaps the only woman on Earth more svelte and trendier is her younger sister Jackie, also known as the "walking syringe," and onetime member of the Baader-Meinhoff gang, who, we learn in one episode, is actually seventy-two

- Saffron, Eddie's ultra-sensible, teetotalling teenage daughter, forever putting up with and mothering her brat of a mother

- Ex-husband Marshall, a former addict and aspiring screen-writer gone Hollywood, and his interchangeable blonde American girlfriends (Bo, an airhead, annoyingly solicitous and forever spouting New Age platitudes; and Cherysh—with a "Y"—a bimbo who says she's "borderline shy, borderline wild," and is proud of her "great tits")

- Ex-husband Justin, Saffron's father, now gay, and his prissy boyfriend, Oliver

- Eddie's mom (June Whitfield)—Saffron's dear old granny—who lives nearby. Pixilated and proper, but with a waspish mean streak herself, she's the constant target of Eddie's abuse, but, always sweetly, gives as good as she gets

- And blissfully buoyant Bubble (Jane Horrocks), Eddie's well-named assistant, forever misremembering and mala-propping, and the only one who dresses more outra-geously than Patsy.

In one typical episode, Patsy arrives at Eddie's on the back of a motorcycle, and announces that she needs to borrow a pair of Eddie's knickers.

"I didn't get home last night."

Marching up and across Eddie's unmade bed in her high heels, black leather jacket, and tight miniskirt, her hair a loose blonde pile perched precariously on her head, Patsy proceeds to rifle through a drawer.

"Do you have any that are G-strings," she asks, holding up a sagging pink silk rectangle, "or are they all jumbo?"

She switched, Eddie admits pathetically, after she caught sight of her backside in a department-store dressing room mirror and thought she might be sharing the cubicle with a sumo wrestler.

The casual drug taking in *Ab Fab*, a comedic affront to one of the most sacred taboos of American television, was very much a part of Patsy and Eddie's lifestyle. The show's theme song was "This Wheel Shall Explode," and its specialty was satirizing that lifestyle, which was a combination of sixties sanctimonious excess with even more sanctimonious eighties and nineties acquisitiveness.

Patsy "worked" (if that was the word for her infrequent pop-ins for champagne swilling at meetings) at a fashion magazine whose denizens specialized in acquiring freebies and scribbling articles that courted potential advertisers, while Eddie owned a little shop that seemed to be forever acquiring craft work at bargain prices from downtrodden Third World countries (African lip plates, for example, resold as ashtrays). It was all, as Eddie repeatedly put it with a dismissive wave, "buggery bollocks."

Stoned on the floor of Eddie's bathroom in one episode, smoking "joss sticks" (as Eddie's mother calls them), Patsy and Eddie fulminate about Morgan Fairchild and Jane Fonda and the "plastic domes on their chests."

Says Eddie heatedly: "There must be a moment about a week after they die when all those women finally achieve the figure they desire!"

In another episode, Eddie comes in late one night after a date with Jean-Pierre, a music video director, and is confronted by Saffron, worried and upset because her mother hadn't called home to say what she'd been doing.

"Too busy doing *it*," Eddie says emphatically, before attacking Saffron for her spinsterish ways. "Not one bloody boyfriend!" she exclaims airily, as sensitive Saffron turns sadly away.

"Here I am, your mother, poised for your first sexual experience, and night after night . . . *dry bloody sheets!*"

"I don't want a mustached virgin for a daughter," Eddie rants, poking Saffron in the back to make her point, "so...*do* something about it."

She pauses, a thought occurs. Eddie's face lights up. "*Unless*, unless of course you're gay," and seeing her daughter's glum face, she jumps ahead, falling practically at her daughter's feet with gratefulness and relief: "Hurrah! Oh, well done!"

"Actually," Saffron snaps tartly, "I'm not. Sorry."

Later, when Patsy and Eddie decide to "have it off," they hire two amateur gigolos for an orgy. They've been recommended by Eddie's gay hairdresser, and the gigolos turn out to be something considerably less than butch. In fact, one of them brings "stiffening spray," which the other mistakenly takes for breath freshener and sprays into his mouth, stiffening his tongue.

It goes without saying that, when the British *Ab Fab* was broadcast in the United States, it became an immediate cult favorite in the American gay community.

TALES OF THE CITY WAS A CHARMING SIX-HOUR 1994 MINISERIES that aired on PBS's *American Playhouse*, and the lives it so sweetly celebrated offended the intolerant and shocked the culturally conservative bourgeoisie.

The miniseries was based on the best-selling novel that in turn was derived from the wildly popular San Francisco newspaper chronicle of life in Baghdad by the Bay in the "anything goes" mid-seventies. It depicted not just sex, but *gay* sex; not merely drugs, but *middle-class people* taking drugs.

Tales was originally financed by British broadcaster Channel 4, the same network that financed daring theatrical films such as *The Crying Game*. It was a sweet-natured, nostalgic fairy tale about a time before AIDS, when spiritual seekers wore leisure suits, landladies offered complementary joints to their tenants, and a good-hearted transsexual could win the heart of a heterosexual captain of industry.

Olympia Dukakis played Mrs. Madrigal, the landlady at 28 Barbary Lane; and the tenants included Chloe Webb as big-haired Mona Ramsey, Paul Gross as womanizing Brian Hawkins, Marcus D'Amico as Michael "Mouse" Tolliver, and Laura Linney as ever-hopeful Mary Ann Singleton.

Tales contained brief nudity, and depicted not only the dread "homosexual lifestyle" that so frightened the social conservatives, but also transsexuality. It caused enough controversy and conservative protest to convince the Corporation for Public Broadcasting that it would be prudent to withdraw from financing the sequel.

OF COURSE, THE BELEAGUERED BROADCAST NETWORKS RE-sponded to the public alarm about the twin evils of sex and violence in the nineties with made-for-television biofilms of both the imprisoned boxer and the set-free football player. They also adapted the stories of other instantly recognizable celebrities and their juicy, sexy, tabloid travails, including Liz, Roseanne, Cher, and Mia, *Peyton Place's* one-time ingenue.

If network prime time seemed at times all but drenched by a dangerous, sexed-up reality, then late night network talk in the mid-nineties remained mostly the province of the celebrity pitchman and the smarmy joke. But sometimes Jay and Dave put aside the shtick and the stupid tricks and battered the fourth wall. Two well-known moments of the period—one on each show—burned the wall right down. "I'm not one to go around blowing my own horn," actor Hugh Grant, who specialized in playing male ingenues, ahemmed with his trademark and winning boyishness in 1995 on *The Tonight Show with Jay Leno*. It was his first public appearance since hiring a Sunset Boulevard prostitute named Divine Brown to perform oral sex on him in his automobile.

The actor's endearing confession of making a mistake earned record ratings for *The Tonight Show* and earned him the forgiveness of the American public and he went right on with his career. He even got to keep his beautiful model-actress girlfriend, Elizabeth Hurley, for a few more years.

On *The Late Show With David Letterman*, Madonna once launched into a diatribe where almost every sentence was bleeped to hide the swear words she used, but it was actress Drew Barrymore, wearing tight black jeans and a clingy powder-blue top bearing the slogan "I'm Bananas Over You," who left the gap-toothed host practically speechless. In an abundance of exuberance during an appearance on the host's birthday, she hopped up on his desk, did an endearing little bump and grind, then pulled up her top and flashed the amazed host with a glimpse of her bare breasts.

"I can't thank you enough for that," he said, for once sounding utterly sincere. "I wish more of our guests would consider that."

The nineties marketplace also responded to concerned parents, who might not want their kids to get even a glimpse of Drew Barrymore's breast, with various, more or less cumbersome "lock-out" devices: the so-called black boxes, retailing for between $75 and $150, that allowed the parents to lock their impressionable kids out of individual programs and time periods, and even out of entire cable channels that aired "inappropriate" programming. But the process required periodic updating and inputting, and constant, active program monitoring by the parents. And that was simply too much button pushing for most folks.

One congressman, high-tech savvy Massachusetts Democrat Ed Markey, allowed that technology was available to build into the new model TV sets, a device to be called the "V-chip." The chip would simplify and automate the entire process of parental viewing supervision, so that it could become a one-touch, one-time operation.

Congress did what it could to respond to voter concerns. That included passage of the Children's Television Act, mandating that local stations air educational shows for kids. There were strong suggestions by powerful politicos, too, that come license-renewal time, the FCC should look unfavorably at stations that aired too much violence. The predictable result in network primetime was less violence and... more sex!

The networks served a new round of sitcom sex talk, on half-hour shows like ABC's *Grace Under Fire* and NBC's *Frasier*, as well as a generous helping of family-friendly hour dramas, shows like *Lois & Clark: The New Adventures of Superman* on ABC, Steven Spielberg's *SeaQuest DSV* on NBC, and *Dr. Quinn: Medicine Woman* on CBS, which nonetheless aired an episode in which a frontier prostitute thought she was pregnant.

Even on a new "gritty" cop show like *NYPD Blue*, the big, scandalous controversy of the fall 1993 season, the issue was not violence, but sex—especially the brief flashes of partial nudity.

VIEWER DISCRETION IS ADVISED.

When it came to raw language and depictions of sexual situations, producer Steven Bochco had been pushing the network TV envelope for years before *NYPD Blue* (1993 to present) debuted. A full decade earlier, in 1983, his *Bay City Blues* included a shot of bare male backsides in a locker-room scene. On his *L.A. Law*, one character was "pissed" at another, while on his short-lived

Cop Rock one character called another a "scumbag." All of this was shocking in its time.

The Reverend Donald Wildmon and his allies mounted a public pressure campaign on *Blue* advertisers long before the premiere episode aired. What incensed them was not only a brief, violent scene with a hooker, but the one minute and five second lovemaking scene between Detective John Kelley (David Caruso) and a female cop (Amy Brenneman), with its brief, warmly lighted glimpses of a bare female breast and buttocks.

Nor did the critics care for exchanges like the one between Kelley and his burned-out partner, Detective Andy Sipowicz (Dennis Franz), who, it's established in the first episode, is a drunk.

"When's the last time you tried goin' on the wagon?" Kelley asks.

Replies Sipowicz: "When's the last time you tried growin' tits?"

But that's how cops talk, the producers protested to the protesters, and the tough language, usually from Sipowicz, just kept coming.

"*Ipsa* this, you pissy little bitch," he snarls once to a female lawyer, grabbing at his crotch, and in another early episode announces, "I'm gonna take a dump."

The first-episode sex scene was a tasteful lovemaking montage with jazzy music and a female voice singing "It's all right, it's all right, c'mon c'mon," and no dialogue.

Kelley, separating after six years of marriage, and Officer Janice Licalsi are seen, in a succession of overlapping dissolves, kissing in the hallway, kissing more passionately inside his apartment, and then Kelley pulls off Licalsi's sweater, leaving her in bra and panties. He then reaches around just below her backside, picks her up, her arms wrapped around his neck, and they fall into his bed. Then we see two naked bodies in shadow. As she rolls into the light, we see a side view of her bare breast, then a clear view of her bare back and butt, then....

Fade out. As disturbing as the critics of sex on television found all this, critics of unreal TV violence also took issue with *NYPD Blue's* first two episodes. In the premiere, Sipowicz is ambushed in a hooker's apartment and shot five times at point-blank range. A week later, in the second episode, he's not only out of the coma and off life support, but back at work—stiff to sure, and walking with the aid of cane, but already his old irascible self.

Despite the criticisms and the initial qualms of advertisers, this Steven Bochco cop show went on to become both a ratings and critical success. Despite the criticism and cast changes—from Caruso to Jimmy Smits to Rick Schroder—its sensibility in the year 2000 remains as edgy as the show's trademark hand-held camerawork.

Meanwhile, elsewhere...

When you get right down to it, nothing made up can be so im-probable, or even so lurid, as ... reality. Not a daytime soap, not even a primetime telenovela.

"Telenovelas," with their nightly "chapters," may run a half year or more and are wildly popular in Latin America—and nowhere more so than in Brazil.

Forty million viewers tuned in every evening in Brazil in 1992 to watch *De Corpo e Alma (Body and Soul)*, for example, the most melodramatic and lurid of any telenovela, and need-less to say, one of the highest rated, as well. It's the obsession-,

continued on next page

continued from previous page

sex-, and violence-filled story of a woman with a heart transplant who falls in love with the lover of her heart's donor.

Twenty-two-year-old Daniella Perez was a featured player in *Corpo e Alma*, albeit a popular one. She played Yasmin, a pretty innocent, whose life was complicated by the attentions of intense and moody Bira, her obsessively jealous boyfriend, played by Guilherme de Padua, an intense and moody young actor in his breakthrough part.

In real life, one morning baby-faced Daniella was found stabbed to death on a roadside on the outskirts of Rio de Janeiro. Soon after, Guilherme de Padua confessed to the crime, but police suspected his pregnant young wife, obsessively jealous herself, may actually have been an accomplice or even committed the murder.

Of course, a love affair gone bad was the most popular theory of the crime, but some analysts also suspected that Guilherme may simply have confused his fictional character with his actual life. Another of the telenovela's many intertwining fictional subplots concerned an older woman's obsessive love for a male stripper. And in real life, too, Guilherme himself had been a male stripper before getting the part.

In yet another soap-opera twist, it turned out that—in real life—Guilherme had been hired by none other than the telenovela's author, Gloria Perez, who was also the murdered starlet's mother! It was she, in fact, who wrote the torrid scenes between her daughter and Guilherme that may have incited the young actor and his jealous wife.

Over the two months after the murder, while the nation was riveted by both *Corpo e Alma* and the unfolding real

continued on next page

continued from previous page

crime story on the nightly news, Gloria Perez continued to write the telenovela's final chapters, right up to its scheduled conclusion, including flashback scenes that featured her murdered daughter.[34]

WHEN IT CAME TO TALKING ABOUT SEX, OR TO SEXUALLY themed story lines, or even to how much skin could be shown, daytime soaps had led the way for most of American TV's first four decades.

In the early 1990s, faced with the new, more explicit competition, the soaps did what they always did best: they turned up the heat. One compilation of the period[35] found the following examples of the new randiness in daytime:

- On ABC's *One Life to Live* a villainous couple played S&M games with a bag of sex "toys"

- On ABC's *General Hospital* the sex game of choice was B&D, with one woman employing her black silk stockings to tie her lover up

- On yet another ABC soap, *Loving*, a sexy woman in lingerie moved her newly paraplegic lover down on their bed so he could perform cunnilingus on her

- Oral sex between a male doctor and his female nurse also was suggested on CBS' *The Young and the Restless*

- And on CBS's *Bold and the Beautiful* the bold plot twist of the day involved one young male character having sex with his beautiful stepmother

But in the nineties there were other, larger social forces at work, and one in particular was washing away that loyal soap audience. Millions of young Generation X and Boomer women, whose mothers had been avid daytime soap watchers, now worked outside the home. Daytime's new talkers, from Montel Williams to Rikki Lake to Jenny Jones to Jerry Springer, went trolling down market for an audience, and they were less inhibited by any old-fashioned notion of decorum. Any sexual kink, no matter how outrageous, seemed fair game for a real-life "theme" show or for a parade of homegrown grotesques.

And when courtrooms opened up to live cameras, what fictional plot could compete with the Kennedy rape case in Florida or the Menendez brothers murder case, or the trial of O.J., or even the impeachment of the president of the United States? So by the end of the decade, the daytime soaps had lost fully one-quarter of their audience. By then Procter & Gamble Productions, the TV division of the premiere soap producer and sponsor, which had once produced a dozen soap operas, was down to just two.

And *Another World*, NBC's longest-running soap and the first to expand to a daily one-hour format, went off the air after thirty-five years and 8,891 episodes.

But if the genre seemed to be dying at the end of the twentieth century, the usual resurrection was just a TV-remote click away. Two all-soap cable channels announced plans to launch early in the new millennium. Their general business plan included rebroadcasting both the past and existing daytime soaps for a nighttime audience.

ONE TOPIC THAT ROILED THE DAYTIME TALK SHOWS IN THE LATER nineties was whether a certain skinny, fictional female lawyer, who was given to pratfalls, mooning about her love life, and wearing miniskirts, was a fit role model for all those millions of young professional women in the work force.

Ally McBeal (Calista Flockhart) even made the cover of *Time* magazine, pictured alongside such actual icons of the feminist movement as Susan B. Anthony, Betty Friedan, and Gloria Steinem. In a headline over Ally/Calista's photograph, the magazine had pointedly asked, "Is Feminism Dead?"

PRACTICALLY EVERYTHING THE LAWYERS AT THE BOSTON FIRM of Cage/Fish & Associates do is, one way or the other, motivated by sex. Of course, Cage/Fish is to *Ally McBeal* (1997 to present) what the bar was to *Cheers*. Of all the lawyers' legal and sexual misadventures, though, the episode with the single funniest punch line is the one in which a nun sues to "get her job back" after being dismissed for violating her vows of celibacy and having a brief but intense affair. In the episode Ally demonstrates convincing orgasm sounds in a conversation with her roommate and friend, and Dyan Cannon, who plays Judge "Whipper" Cone, is briefly seen nude in full-figure profile. But the kicker to the tale of the wayward nun is this: A priest turns out to have been secretly videotaping confessions (including the nun's) to fulfill his ambition of becoming a Fox TV producer—of *The World's Naughtiest Confessions*, we are told!

It was, quite possibly, the funniest inside dig at a network by a show that airs on it since Homer and Marge Simpson, watching television at home in Springfield, wondered deadpan how come they hadn't noticed it when Fox changed over to a hardcore sex channel.

TRASH TV? HARDLY! IT'S SIMPLY REALITY.

So said the supporters of the New Thing, as it snowballed out of the late 1980s and on through the nineties. Those supporters pointed out that "reality," "infotainment," "checkbook journalism," "confrontational" talk shows, and "magazine-style" programming—whatever you wanted to call the new mix of talk and news and titillation—was, bottom line, simply cheaper to produce. Indeed, it was so cost effective that it tended to drive other genres off the air.

By 1990 everybody seemed to have a minicam and so anybody was a "source" for the New Thing. In media circles, the decade of the 1990s was bracketed, and the limits of prime-time series programming were to some degree defined, by home taping.

Sordid crime and blatant sex—often raw and kinky, and with no noticeable redeeming value—led the nightly evening *network* news. From actor Rob Lowe, who ignited a media furor in 1989 after he taped himself having three-way sex including a sixteen-year-old girl he'd picked up in an Atlanta club, to the much-reviled Linda Tripp, who in 1998 secretly audiotaped her young friend talking about fellating the president of the United States—all of this was regular network fare.

At the beginning of the nineties, Lowe was simply a pin-up teen actor, the Leonardo DiCaprio of his time; by the end of the decade, he was a seasoned actor and a regular on NBC's *The West Wing*, playing Sam Seaborn, the White House's deputy communications director. In the pilot episode—in what was doubtless a wry reference to Lowe's own scandalous background—he "accidentally" sleeps with a call girl.

Early in the nineties, the three Amy Fisher TV movies marked something of a watershed: all were about something tawdry and lurid, but all had high ratings. Clearly, Americans liked to watch.

By the middle of the decade, the Family Hour was no longer

sacrosanct. Both *Cybill* and *Roseanne* were moved to 8 P.M., where they were briefly joined by a sitcom starring Andrew "Dice" Clay, a comic who'd made his mark with an act that presented him as a scathingly (and scatologically) unreconstructed blue-collar male chauvinist. In fact, sex talk and sexual situations were so common-place in prime time that an ostensibly family-friendly CBS sitcom like *The Nanny* could trade in sexy double entendres (such as the difference between the Nanny's randy grandmother, her *bubbe*, and the Nanny's boobies) and show the title character (Fran Drescher) drunk, mistakenly stumbling into bed with her boss, then waking up the next morning unable to remember whether they'd had sex or not. (The boss didn't know either.) And on the national evening news, each sexual mention, even if circumspect or clinical, by Rather, Jennings, and Brokaw shook the temple of established social convention and propriety that much more.

What was "decent" and "seemly" to show and talk about on the air became not only more difficult to articulate—community *standards?*—but increasingly irrelevant. Until by the 1999 season, *The Practice,* a prime-time dramatic series on Disney-owned ABC, seemed to define the current line when the writers, at the network's request, substituted the word "fellatio" in a script for their original preference, "blow job."

If that was one step over the edge when it came to language, then what was a matter of course on network television still was shocking as an alien plot to some. For example, in one early summer edition of ABC's *Nightline,* just after the end of the war between NATO and Yugoslavia, no less a personage than TV newsman Ted Koppel felt it was within bounds to tell one Serbian interviewee, a Kosovo tavern owner, that his initial answer about atrocities had been "bullshit."[36]

In one single brief speech on one prime-time episode of Fox's

The X-Files, to cite another typical example, Agent Mulder said both "piss–poor" and "duck's ass."[37] And in another example of just where the various networks thought the line of what was acceptable should be drawn, CBS objected to a sentence in an episode of its *L.A. Doctors* series that read: "The only parts that work are your brain and your schlong." The producers changed the word "schlong" to "johnson" and the line aired.

Four decades before, that kind of talk would have caused outrage in the halls of the United States Congress. Just a few years before, the network and the advertisers would have been deluged by protests organized by the Reverends Wildmon and Falwell, as they were earlier in the decade when ABC aired a *thirtysomething* episode showing two men together in bed. (The network lost approximately one million dollars in advertising revenue as a result, then opted not to air that particular episode as a rerun.)

In the late 1990s, the "johnson" line went out on the broadcast airwaves of the most mainstream-minded network without a ripple of notice. Of course, the political story of the decade, the impeachment of the president, was all about blow jobs, too. By the 2000 political season, to take one typical example, David Letterman could refer to Bob Jones University (controversial in the campaign because of its ban on interracial dating and its founder's belief that Catholicism is a satanic cult) as B.J. U. That was where Monica went to school, he observed drolly, to big, knowing laughs.

ON "PREMIUM" CABLE IN THE NINETIES, BOTH HBO AND SHOWtime were producing stylish, sophisticated fare, including original movies that not only often had partial nudity and sexy plots, but were budgeted higher than their broadcast-network counterparts, as well as such series as *The Garry Shandling Show, The Sopranos, Sex and the City,* and *Queer as Folk,* Showtime's new series (still in the planning stage at this writing) about a group of gay men, including a sexually active teenager.

As early as the mid 1980s, Cinemax had begun airing occasional *Eros America* documentaries. That subject matter was taken up by HBO in 1990 on its late night one-hour news magazine *Real Sex* specials, produced by an *Eros* co-creator. The high-rated *Real Sex* usually included five segments interspersed with funny and titillating interviews with people on the street. Over the years, subjects have included naked group sex therapy sessions for couples, customized S&M Barbie dolls, sex toys, strippers at the venerable Crazy Horse in Paris, a "finishing school" for male cross dressers, erotic CD-ROMS, and a popular Brazilian performer who, adorned only by glittery body paint, dances naked through the packed streets of Rio at the height of Carnival.

For the sophisticated young women of *Sex and the City* (1998 to present), dancing through the streets, naked under those strategic daubs of body paint, might be merely another intriguing fashion statement. This may be the first show in which young women really talk just the way they do in real life—provided that in real life they're painfully literate Manhattan sophisticates—about relationships and sex, and about men and their many shortcomings. Or is it just another male sitcom fantasy, distinguished by uncommonly direct (or crude and crass, if you prefer) sex talk and fleeting glimpses of frontal nudity?

Well, its creator's credits do include *Beverly Hills 90210* and *Melrose Place*, hardly models of tough social realism, but it also has Merrill Markoe, David Letterman's ex-head writer and ex-girlfriend, as a consultant. It's also undeniably funny and its female quartet's observations about men and relationships and sex and, yes, the city are undeniably trenchant and thought-provoking. For example: Getting over a break-up takes exactly half the length of time the relationship lasted. Sounds about right, doesn't it? Occasionally the episodes are even poignant.

Much of the credit for that has to go to Sarah Jessica Parker, who so splendidly plays Carrie Bradshaw, a newspaper sex columnist, or "sexpert" as she's called in a society column after she goes out with a new player for the New York Yankees.

Carrie's "research" consists of living as a contemporary young single woman in Manhattan and hanging out in restaurants and coffee shops and dishing with her three upscale female friends—Samantha (Kim Cattrall), a public relations executive, Miranda (Cynthia Nixon), a lawyer, and Charlotte (Kristin Davis), an art dealer. One dates a man with a tiny penis, another's boyfriend is a "ball player," constantly grabbing at himself and adjusting his "package" in public. Perhaps he's a "low hanger," the women speculate, and Samantha recalls hearing that actor Nick Nolte once had a "ball lift."

Later, we see Samantha and her poorly endowed boyfriend doing it in a variety of positions. "Fuck me, fuck me, you hot stud!" she cries out, encouraging him to perform, before finally giving up and, much to his dismay, turning on her vibrator. Later, perhaps inevitably, they find themselves hemming and hawing about the actual "issue" of his inadequate penis to a trendy, silver-haired therapist.

Other men in these post-feminist women's lives get nicknames like Mr. Marvelous and Mr. Pussy, who's an expert cunnilinguist, and the never-named "Mr. Big," the one man Carrie can't seem to get over. (The show is based on Candace Bushnell's "Sex and the City" columns in the New York Observer newspaper, and Mr. Big, it turns out, is based on Vogue's publisher, Ronald A. Galotti, whom Ms. Bushnell once dated.[38])

If there's one obsession that rivals relationships for the four Sex women, it's fashion, and the show is a veritable pageant of Gucci, Dolce & Gabbana, and whichever downtown Manhattan clothing designer is à la mode.

"It's like seventh grade with bank accounts," says Miranda to her friends at one point, exasperated by the constant chatter about men at their movable Algonquin Round Table of graphic and epigrammatic sex talk.

If the show has a false note, it's that the women seem always to be returning to a fetish with penis size, which seems less like a daring insight and more like a reflection of the sensibility of the show's male writers. In its larger cultural context (and, yes, it does have one), *Sex and the City* is another example of Girl Power, the same pop phenomenon behind the success of films like *Titanic*, novels like *Bridget Jones's Diary* and, of course, the welcome rise in popularity of women's soccer, basketball, and other sports.

And given the four central characters' ever-ready randiness, and their obsessions with relationships that never seem to work out, as well as with fashion and all things hip, the HBO show is more than just casually reminiscent of Britain's taboo-breaking, and very politically incorrect, *Absolutely Fabulous*. The *Sex and the City* women, who'd probably prefer to be called girls anyway, even call each other "sweetie" and smoke and drink too much.

AS FAR BACK AS THE MID-SEVENTIES, HOLLYWOOD STUDIO THEatrical movies had begun to give themselves almost entirely to the "blockbuster" mentality, and to increasingly empty spectacle. The trend only accelerated with the computer-driven special effects technology of the nineties. Big, "novelistic" theatrical movies, like *The Godfather* pictures, and miniseries, the so-called "novels for television," like *Roots*, seemed destined to become casualties of the cult of spectacle and the constrictions of the bottom line.

Where once there was strict demarcation between those who did TV and those who did films, in the nineties that distinction collapsed. Movies, from *Dragnet* to *The Mod Squad* and *Mission: Impossible*, looked like "classic" TV with big-screen effects, while TV shows could aspire to the texture, depth, and operatic tapestry of *The Godfather*.

When HBO did its own Mafia saga, there were differences, of course. The language was tougher, the violence more graphic, and the nudity more casual and complete. It was *The Godfather* with angst and analysis. You don't have to be mobbed up (though it might help to have friends in Cherry Hills), to know *The Sopranos* (1999 to present), the critical darling of television, is absolutely faithful to its New Jersey roots.

There's Tony Soprano (James Gandolfini), the mob boss, who insists he's in waste management and the Mafia is nothing but a media myth. Tony has stress. He's trying to do the right thing, live by the code, balance his family with his Family, his wife with his sexy young Russian mistress.

Then there are the desultory topless strippers, the hot-blooded young Mafia soldiers, even a "sensitive" priest named Father Phil, who loves movies and ziti, and who turns Carmela Soprano's (Edie Falco) communion into a seduction technique. There's even the capo who likes to do Al Pacino imitations and quote lines of dialogue from *The Godfather*. Is it any wonder Tony is taking Prozac (though it does render him impotent in one episode when his mistress tries giving him oral sex)?

The violence is quick, brutish, and authentic—it's just business, after all—and so is the sex. In one episode mob boss Tony, who's seeing a therapist because of his anxiety attacks, beats a man nearly to death; in another he garrotes a mob turncoat. In yet another he brings a "nurse" to a sick friend in the hospital. Actually, the sexy girl in the too-tight nurse's uniform is a dancer from his strip club. She does a little bump and grind and shrugs out of her nurse's costume. Topless, nipples erect, wearing only a thong, she licks the sick man's neck. "Time for your sponge bath," she says.

A decade earlier, Roseanne had baited the censors with "pitching the trouser tent" and other colorful synonyms for "erection." In its second season finale, in April 2000, *The Sopranos* included a dream sequence in which Tony's trouser-tented erection was quite clearly noticeable, poking up and out under the front pleat of his pants. Would-be censors seemed to be looking elsewhere.

This time the adoring critics are right: this HBO series, created by a refugee from *Northern Exposure*, with a writer-producer team from that series as well, is among the best ever to air on American TV.

HOW COULD THE BROADCAST NETWORKS COPE WITH THE UNFET-tered sex and violence on pay TV when they couldn't even keep UPN and the WB, the new "weblets" (as *Variety* calls them), as well as all those other new media competitors for eyeballs and dollars, from luring away the most demographically desirable parts of the audience?

The competition on the new, quasi-networks, on (basic) cable and (made-for) video targets ever-smaller niche audiences, often teens and younger, who, according to the programmers, are more apt to tune in for a steady diet of gross out schoolyard humor, ultra-violence and other, more sensationalistic and cheaper thrills.

On UPN, for example, that meant *WWF Smackdown* and the return of professional wrestling to prime-time TV. And that meant the salvation of UPN, once considered a weak competitor that was on the endangered species list, which promptly registered a 35 percent jump in its ratings, thanks to wrestling. On the WB that meant teenage girls with superpowers or teens with super angst.

Kids since the days of Bram Stoker have known there's something sexy about the idea of bloodsucking vampires. Case in point, *Buffy the Vampire Slayer* (1999 to present).

The 1999 season-ending *Buffy* episode, withheld for months because its original air date fell too near the infamous Columbine High School shootings, turned out to contain only mild fantasy violence. But it did have a very nicely sexed-up bloodsucking scene in which shirtless Angel (David Boreanaz), a good vampire (so good, in fact, that he even got his own spin-off show), "feeds" on Buffy (Sarah Michelle Gellar), who hooks her legs around him while they thrash around suggestively on the floor.

It's merely entertainment, said the producers, disclaiming any larger social significance. But you don't have to be a kid who dresses goth to think this episode was *very* educational TV.

ON FOX, MEANWHILE, WHICH HAD COME TO RELY EVER MORE ON "stunts" and special "reality" programming of the *When Animals Attack* kind, the pursuit of kids with disposable income meant a brief flirtation with a sitcom sensibility that echoed what was working so well in big-screen movies such as *Something About Mary* and *American Pie:* "This is all happening because society is evolving and changing," Doug Herzog, then the president of Fox Entertainment, who had formerly headed Comedy Central, where he'd greenlighted a show called *South Park*, said of his new 1999–2000 season series. "But the bottom line is, people seem to be buying it."[39]

There were highly touted shows like *Action*, a half-hour satire of Hollywood moviemaking, which marked one of the first times on broadcast television that obscenities and epithets were spoken by the characters, but bleeped out, which still left them easy enough to lip-read. *Action* was produced by a real Hollywood action movie producer, Joel Silver *(Die Hard, Predator,* and many others), and it revolved around the aptly named Peter Dragon, an arrogant and abusive (and insecure) fictional Hollywood producer of action movies (played by Jay Mohr). He browbeat his subordinates, hired a hooker as a development executive (played by Ileana Douglas), and "took a pitch" from an agent (played by a well-known real agent, in an insider cameo) who offered his client, O. J. Simpson, to him for a role in a movie.

Critics loved it, though they wondered if the humor was too inside and too uneven, and if the lack of any good guy to root for would be a problem. So high were the expectations for *Action* that Fox built its entire 1999 fall season promotional campaign around it. But despite the critical raves, and despite cameos by movie stars like Sandra Bullock and Keanu Reeves, audiences never bothered to tune in, and—shortly after the obligatory expression of firm support by network executives—the show was cancelled, replaced by a game show. Only eight episodes had aired.

Manchester Prep, also scheduled for Fox's new 1999–2000 season, never even had a single episode air. It was to have been a TV version of *Cruel Intentions*, the big-screen teenage version of *Dangerous Liaisons*—complete with disparaged virgins and seductive vixens—and one of several big-screen versions of *Les Liaisons Dangereuses*, an eighteenth-century novel about elaborate sex games among the debauched nobility.

While the ratings were disastrous for Fox's new fall series, a modest "summer replacement" on ABC called *Who Wants to Be a Millionaire* was becoming a runaway hit. So potent in the ratings was *Millionaire* that ABC network executives scrambled to cancel sitcoms that in other years they would've kept on the schedule (for example, *It's Like, You Know . . .*), just to make room for additional *Millionaire* airings.

The conventional wisdom had been that only older, less demographically desirable audiences would watch game shows. *Millionaire* shattered that shibboleth. The whole family was gathering to watch, turning the various time periods during which it aired into de facto family hours, and *Millionaire's* advertising rates quickly ascended to the stratosphere, becoming among the highest in all of TV. In the space of a few short weeks at the end of 1999 and early in 2000, *Millionaire* singlehandedly raised ABC from third to first place and in sight of renewed profitability.

In fact, almost solely on the strength of repeated *Millionaire* airings, ABC won the February 2000 sweeps, both in total viewers and in adults aged eighteen to forty-nine, the most desirable demographic. It was the network's first February win in twelve years. The Alphabet Network's longest previous winning streak—fourteen straight weeks at number one during the 1978–79 season—was in the era of *Happy Days* and the other Marshall comedies. With the whole country chanting along as Regis Philbin intoned "Is that your final answer?," that record was soon eclipsed. Critics at the other networks immediately cried foul, pointing out that fully 18 percent of ABC's primetime February sweeps schedule—sixteen hours—was not regular series programming, but had been given over to *Millionaire* broadcasts, some scheduled on short notice. Harmed the most by ABC's game show juggernaut was Fox, which saw its own sweeps ratings drop by around 9 percent.

Statistics like that set off a stampede to revive the genre, moribund since the quiz show scandals of the late fifties. The first new quiz show to make it on the air was Fox's aptly titled *Greed*, hosted by Chuck Woolery, which, appropriately enough replaced *Action* on the schedule; the second was NBC's revival of *Twenty-One*, the same quiz that had brought the genre down in the fifties, hosted by Maury Povich. Both started out with big ratings, and by early in 2000, each of the Big Four networks was airing its own prime time game show.

SITCOMS, WENT THE NEW CONVENTIONAL WISDOM ONCE AGAIN, were now played out and dead. Soon, Hollywood's television writers, anxious in the best of times, were worrying over cappuccinos that the deluge of game shows that was surely coming would mean less "shelf space" on the networks' schedules for sitcoms and dramas of the sort they wrote: and in turn *that* would mean an increase in unemployment—not for just writers, but for anyone who had a job in series TV.

At Fox, a new executive was swiftly brought in to oversee the new network president whose first six new series, the entire fall slate, had failed so spectacularly. Weeks later, though, just when critics and execs were getting comfortable with the new consensus, *Malcolm in the Middle*, a smart new take on the traditional "family" sitcom that was one of the final parts of that schedule, debuted on Fox.

In its opening episode, the father stood naked in the kitchen (reading a newspaper that covered his private parts) so Mom could shave his back, while the kids nonchalantly continued to eat breakfast. In another episode Malcolm, the middle child of this all-American and eccentric nuclear family, spotted Dad coming out of a porn store. In yet another, Mom and Dad are frustrated by the lack of privacy after they're forced into close quarters with the kids while their house is being fumigated. Unable to find anywhere else to make love, they finally don gas masks and stroll hand in hand into the fumigation tent, disappearing inside a poisonous white cloud. The show, which dispensed with a laugh track, didn't have the look or feel of most sitcoms (because it wasn't shot like them, with the traditional three cameras on a sound stage in front of a studio audience), and was instantly both a critical and ratings success. Suddenly, miraculously, the "dead" sitcom genre had revived. At that point, the president of Fox Entertainment, who'd bought the show for the network, might have been excused for crowing, "You're not the boss of me!"—the refrain from the *Malcolm* theme song. But by then it was too late: within a few weeks, he was out, replaced in fact by the production company executive responsible for *Malcolm*.

By the time you hold this book in your hand, *Malcolm* undoubtedly will have been cloned countless times for ABC, CBS, and NBC.

THE NEW LICENSE OF THE LATE NINETIES MEANT NEW CREATIVE freedom for prime time's creators. And, arguably, the last decade of the second millennium was something of a TV programming renaissance at the Big Three networks, as they sought to keep that mass—but no longer monolithic—audience from defecting. The Big Three did this while, of course, relentlessly targeting the young adults, most desirable to advertisers.

With entire broadcast networks specializing in programs for audiences comprised only of teens and twentysomethings, what better way could there be to reach those "young adults" than to show the kids on TV thinking about having sex, talking about sex and—but usually only during sweeps months—actually having it?

The trend toward sexed-up programming aimed directly at kids got underway in earnest early in the last decade. In a 1991 episode of *Beverly Hills, 90210*, for example, Brenda finally had sex with Dylan (but soon regretted it), and that same year on *Doogie*

Howser, M.D., the teenage doctor turned eighteen and lost his virginity. In one 1992–1993 season episode of the critically acclaimed *Picket Fences*, two giggly teenage girls, experimenting, kissed each other. A survey of the most popular shows that year among children seventeen and under found that, "on average, 29 percent of all interactions involved sex talk of some kind. *Blossom* at 58 percent and *Martin* at 49 percent led the pack."[40]

As the nineties continued, more new networks, both over the air and cable, emerged, and often their programming was targeted resolutely at the young, so that by the end of the decade their schedules were seemingly obsessed with "it" every hour of every prime-time night.

BY THE LATE NINETIES, IT WAS NO BIG DEAL WHEN BOTH BUFFY and Felicity, the teenaged title characters of two favorite TV shows among teens, lost their virginity, but it seems that even as far back as the 1970s, kids were obsessed with sex.

Who knew?! Adults back then tuned in to *The Brady Bunch* kids, who were smiling cutely and pouting prettily, and getting into all kinds of inconsequential scrapes. They probably never dreamed they were being mocked by another group of teens sitting around a basement rec room, stoned, in mid-seventies Point Place, Wisconsin, the setting of Fox's *That '70s Show* (1998 to present).

It was the boogie nights era of bell bottoms, happy faces, the gas crisis, and *Rocky*. The kids, like real kids everywhere, were working on their night moves (and Eric was working on getting Donna's bra off), and, of course, they were playing Pong while listening to the Who.

That '70s Show's alternate working titles, *The Kids Are Alright* and *Teenage Wasteland,* are fairly good indicators of its creators' intent.

If the Bundys were not the Cosbys, then surely Eric and Donna, Kelso and Jackie, Fes (whose name is an acronym for Foreign Exchange Student), and Hyde, the stoner with the sideburns and the hair (the one who's partial to tinted glasses and Jimmy Page T-shirts), are the anti-Bradys. And that goes for Laurie, Eric's older sister, too, who wears her hair in a Farrah Fawcett shag, looks like a Brady gone bad, and exhibits the disdainful worldliness that only comes from an entire semester away at college.

In fact, in the show's very first episode, Jackie (Mila Kunis), Michael Kelso's button-cute girlfriend, is intently watching Marcia on TV while the rest of the kids talk about an upcoming Todd Rundgren concert.

Jackie herself exists in a sitcom simulacrum of the real seventies, that post-sixties disco interlude when "love" was still free and sex was still revolutionary rather than dangerous. But she's very much in the Brady mold. And like real kids of the period, she's not above using her sexual allure to get a boyfriend—in her case, Kelso (Ashton Kutcher), the self-involved jock and doofus of the bunch—and after a few episodes of this gentle, well-written satire, she and Kelso have had sex and she confides to Donna that she fears she's pregnant.

Like real kids, the '70s Show teens like to dance (the hustle), listen to music (Led Zeppelin), drink beer and smoke pot (when they can score it) and, especially, make out. And the kids like watching TV, from which they learn the usual life lessons.

"Who knew," says Fes (Wilmer Valderrama) with his faint lisp and generic Third World accent, looking up from an afternoon special everybody's watching in Eric's basement, "that it takes only one beer to turn a cheerleader into a harlot!"

The series high point thus far, and its most determinedly anti-Brady episode, was the second-season opener, in which Eric (Topher Grace) was traumatized into denial by a glimpse of his parents, Red and Kitty, having sex. Afterward, at the dinner table, he can't even bring himself to look at them because when he does he imagines them sitting there naked, his mother taking dainty bites from a sausage. At night, Eric can't sleep, tossing and turning, while his parents' coital moans—"Oh Kitty, Oh Kitty!" and "Oh Red, Red!"—echo in his brain.

"Make it stop!" he cries out.

Of course, Kitty (Debra Jo Rupp) and Red (Kurtwood Smith) notice this peculiar behavior, and like the good anti-Bradys they are, immediately conclude that their son is "on dope."

When Eric confides in red-haired Donna (Laura Prepon), the bright, self-possessed and generally obliging next door girl of his dreams, explaining to her why he's not in the mood to make out in the parked car, she replies with the story of her own childhood trauma. At age twelve seeing her parents doing "it" outside on the hammock, in broad daylight, in the very place where she innocently read her Nancy Drew books! Then later, she remembers, "they had this checkerboard pattern all over their arms and legs." Of course, just thinking about Donna's sexy mother (played by Tanya Roberts, a former *Charlie's Angel*) puts Eric right back in the mood, but by then it's too late.

"You've been extra loserly lately," Eric's big sister scoffs at another point, so he confides in her, too: "They were like a pair of wildebeests on a National Geographic special!" he says, still aghast, and its part of this series' wacky charm that we immediately see a nature-special sketch, complete with portentous voice-over announcer, about Red and Kitty's mating behavior. Naturally, Laurie snitches.

Kitty, a nurse, is relieved her son isn't on drugs; Red is faintly embarrassed. Urged on by his wife to give their son some appropriate words of advice, he simply says, "It's more fun than it looks."

It's advice Eric and Donna take to heart, just in time for the February 2000 sweeps, finally doing it and losing their virginity with an endearing and comic awkwardness.

THE PURSUIT OF THE NEW AND THE TITILLATING THROUGHOUT the nineties meant unprecedented genre-bending on both broadcast and basic cable networks, and the new ingredient in the new hybrids invariably turned out to be *sex*.

Where once there were game shows, whether silly or serious, now there were innuendo-filled contests like the syndicated *Personals* and *Studs*, MTV's *The Blame Game*, and USA's *Strip Poker*.

Where once there were fictional soaps and real documentaries, now there were quasi-documentaries with soap opera elements and real people whose real sexual affairs were chronicled by omnipresent TV cameras, shows like MTV's *Real World* and *Road Rules*.

And where once there were cartoons, now there were very adult cartoons, such as *The Simpsons* and, on cable, *South Park*.

And as the odometer on the wired planet clicked over to 2000, the proliferating, conglomerating, all-consuming, on-all-the-time "media" made certain these trends would continue.

Meanwhile, elsewhere...

In the wild, wild east of post-Soviet Russia, the nightly prime time Siberian tractor report was history; American-style TV news was all the rage.

continued on next page

continued from previous page

In 1999, when Yuri Skuratov, Russia's top prosecutor, an anti-corruption crusader and the shining light of the anti-government opposition, suddenly resigned, allegedly for health reasons, it shocked both his supporters and his opponents in the polarized and cutthroat world of Moscow politics.

But when he returned, just as suddenly, a few weeks later to announce publicly that he would fight to regain his old job, Russia's Byzantine political maneuvering and underground political pressures erupted into televised scandal.

On a government-controlled TV channel, a late night news program aired a brief black-and-white videotape in which the married forty-six-year-old Skuratov appeared naked, frolicking in bed with two naked young women, neither of whom was his wife.

Reportedly, that video had been taped more than a year earlier in a Moscow apartment belonging to an individual in Skuratov's office with ties to powerful local bankers.

"There are two conclusions you can draw from this," a radio commentator and former press secretary to President Boris Yeltsin said of the entire affair. "The first is that there are no politics in Russia, only political intrigues. And the second is that everyone has compromising material on everyone else, and usually, it is true."[41]

Perhaps there is a third conclusion to be drawn, the one that seems to have been drawn by an enterprising Russian news producer. Early in 2000, a TV news show called *The Naked Truth* (with no known connection to the former NBC sitcom of the same name) began to air in Russia. On it, a pretty

continued on next page

continued from previous page

female newsreader strips, button by button, while reading a digest of the day's events. The show, needless to say, is wildly popular,[42] and doubtlessly is being eyed even now as a possible new format for the increasingly sensationalistic and celebrity-driven American local TV news.

CONTRARY TO THE OPINION OF A CERTAIN FOURTH-GRADE teacher on *South Park* (1997 to present), the high point of sex on television so far has not been Chad Everett. But it conceivably could be this adult cartoon series, about a bunch of eight-year-old children living in a mountain hamlet in Colorado.

Not only is Eric Cartman's sweet-voiced mom a hermaphrodite crack whore, but pudgy little Eric himself has the most politically incorrect opinions to be found anywhere on television. His views would give pause even to *Ally McBeal's* Richard Fish.

What, Eric's teacher asks in one episode, is the definition of sexual harassment? Cartman immediately pipes up that it's "when you're having sex with your lady friend and some other guy comes up and tickles your balls from behind."

Naturally, when his little friend Stan pronounces him an "ass sucker," Eric proceeds to sue him for sexual harassment. In the ensuing trial, their deeply disturbed teacher Mr. Garrison, who's adamant about not being gay but whose most intimate relationship is with a puppet named Mr. Hat, calls the judge "toots" and "baby."

Eric is represented in court by his other friend's father, attorney Gerald Broflofski, a devout, yarmulka-wearing Jew, who wins so many millions representing children in sexual harassment suits that he bankrupts the South Park school district. He even takes to

TV in a commercial, urging kids who have been called "homo," "farty pants," or "butt face" to sue.

Eric doesn't likes hippies or poor people and thinks a woman's place is in the kitchen, fixing him beefy roast and cheesy poofs, and he most definitely tends to go to extremes to get his way. In one memorable two-part episode, when he demanded to know who his father was, his sweet-voiced mom first explains the process of procreation ("the man puts his hoo-hoo-dilly in the woman's cha-cha") before launching into a reminiscence of the events that occurred at a certain annual drunken barn dance.

That was the dreamy night, it turns out, that Cartman's mom had sex with just about every man in the greater South Park environs, including Chief Running Water, who calls her "Bear With Wide Canyon," Chef (whose deep, sexy voice is provided by Isaac Hayes), and the entire 1991 Denver Broncos football team.

Genetic testing provides the improbable answer: Cartman's father turns out to Cartman's mother, who turns out to be a hermaphrodite. But that's not even *South Park's* most outrageous plot twisting of sex and DNA.

In another episode, Kyle decides to use gene splicing to combine elephant DNA with the DNA of Fluffy, Eric's pet pot-bellied pig, in order to create a more conveniently sized elephant. But since it transpires that pig and elephant DNA just won't splice, the kids do what they always do when they need some good advice, they go to Chef, who offers his all-purpose answer:

Get the pig and the elephant to "make sweet love."

"And how do you that?" the kids ask back.

"Get 'em good and drunk," Chef says. And later, when the inebriated elephant mounts the drunken pig, Chef is moved to remark, "Hmm, now I know how all those white women felt."

The next day, the pig gives birth in class, and the little baby pig looks like Mr. Garrison. To which Cartman, echoing the most famous line in the film *Babe*, says, "That'll do, pig."

Along with the kids, their parents, Principal Victoria, Mr. Garrison, and Mr. Mackey ("mm-kay"), *South Park* regulars include both Jesus, who has a local cable access show called *Jesus and Pals*, and Satan, who has a boxing match with the Prince of Peace (of course, Satan throws the fight). Satan's son even shows up at the elementary school in an *Omen*-like satire.

The show gleefully skewers targets all across the political-correctness spectrum. It manages to satirize both gay people and the rain forest in just one episode about the misadventures of the South Park kids on a field trip to Costa Rica. In this one they're an Up With People-style singing and dancing group called Get Gay With Kids, and, of course, the lesson they learn from their encounters with wild animals and the aboriginal natives is that the rain forest is dangerous and should be destroyed.

Another episode tosses around the implications of Kyle and Stan's dads masturbating together in a hot tub and draws the conclusion that everyone does it and everyone's a little bit gay. There's even a fey occasional character called Big Gay Al, who turns up to shelter South Park's outcast gay animals.

It's easy to forget that these inexplicably expressive cutout characters in the wickedly funny plots are mere cartoons, but then that was true of *Monty Python*'s animation, too.

BY THE LATE NINETIES THE INTERNET BOOM WAS WELL UNDERWAY. Another new medium arises to challenge the old, fueled yet again by the combination of technological innovation and good old-fashioned pornography. This time it's delivered into the home via the Mac and the PC, the modem and the World Wide Web.

A couple of decades before, porn on video had fueled the VCR boom, just as porn-on-pay had fueled the cable TV boom; this time around, many of the newly empowered "Netizens" were surfing the Web looking for dirty pictures and hardcore "streaming" action, as well as electronic bulletin boards and chat rooms where they could obsess about sex. "After the techno-nerds came the techno-pervs," one wag said of the first waves of Net growth, and both times they were just the same teenage boys.

In fact, one academic study estimated that as many as one-third of all net surfers headed for sexually-oriented sites. Another survey, sponsored by the National Center for Missing & Exploited Children, found that approximately one in five kids between the ages of ten and seventeen who were regular users of the Internet in 1999 received a sexual solicitation. That potentially dire circumstance was played for laughs in an episode of *Ally McBeal,* in which Ally is arrested for statutory rape after unwittingly have computer sex with a sixteen-year-old boy.

As the nineties went on, broadcast-network aggregate viewing levels, which had once been 90-plus percent in the Big Three network days, fell to around half the potential audience, with viewers defecting by the millions to cable and home video's racier programming, and to their interactive and readily X-rated computer screens.

If the traditional broadcast networks, the Big Three plus Fox, needed any additional impetus beyond their more daring and less restricted competitors to go farther, to throw standards and caution to the winds of change, they had to look no farther than the evening news in 1998 and 1999, where each night brought new stories about trysts in the Oval Office, semen stains, oral sex, and erotic uses of cigars imaginative enough to do Freud himself proud.

On the last Academy Awards telecast of the 1990s, host Whoopi Goldberg, in her opening monologue on what is one of the most

watched TV shows of any year, blithely summarized the presidential scandal in a way that demonstrated exactly what was considered suitable for the largest audience broadcast television could
still summon: "I feel the need to get all this out of my system
right now," she said at the top of the show, "so here goes: subpoenas, cigars. Black berets, DNA. Intern, rug burns. Henry Hyde,
gratified. Prime-time confession, jury in session. Mr. Trent Lott,
out, out, damn spot.

"Talking points, approval ratings, phone sex, dating. Stop
hanging out in Betty Currie's driveway, I mean, let that bitch get
into her car!"

And without the late nineties presidential sex scandal to make
comic references to blow jobs acceptable, would there ever have
been a sketch on late night's *Mad TV* like the one about the husband who grabs the back of his wife's head, pushing her down,
every time she makes even the most innocent reference to oral
sex? That sketch ended with the husband calling in the family cat,
"Here, puss, puss," at which point the wife leaps at him, grabbing
the back of *his* head.

The Future
of Television

Liking to Look, Looking to Converge

ELABORATE WRESTLING SPECTACLES! BIG BUCKS GAME SHOWS! News (so squishy soft that it should be called "infotainment") and unabashed voyeurism, all of which are designed to appeal to the young. And for the first time in forty years, the return to prime time of live, movie-length theatrical drama, with a production of the Cold-War-era doomsday thriller *Fail Safe*. On Wall Street and in American society at large, the triumphalism of a new Gilded Age.

In network executive suites a maddened pursuit of ever younger viewers, shakily counter-balanced to some extent by the rediscovery of a large (and aging) adult audience, which will tune in for such well-crafted dramas such as *Family Law, Judging Amy, Once and Again, Providence,* and *The West Wing*. Not only has *The Fugitive* come back to network television, but the most fashionable segments of its audience are dressing retro, in Capri pants or Clark Desert Boots, too.

Welcome (back) to the (near term) future of television. History seems to be repeating itself all right, only this time it's digitized and better armed, with more disposable income and Net access.

The birth of the medium of television coincided with the birth of the Baby Boomers. At the time, they were the biggest single generation of kids since the founding of the Republic. The birth of computers and the medium of cyberspace coincided with the birth of the Digital Generation (or Gen Y, if you prefer), the children, and sometimes the grandchildren, of the original Boomers.

Born between 1977 and 1997, the eighty-one million Digital kids are the largest generation ever, bigger even than the Boomers. In the year 2000 their aggregate consumer spending power is estimated at between $150 billion to $250 billion per year, with about a third of that going to clothes.[43] And these kids have grown up with cable and videos, videogames, PlayStation, cell phones and pagers, satellite dishes, computers, modems, printers and scanners, and all manner of other nifty peripherals in the house. These kids also have every imaginable kind of hard-core pornography readily downloadable, not to mention everything from bomb-making instructions to methamphetamine recipes, right there on the Web, just a mouse click away.

Adults fear these wised-up, sped-up, wired-up kids; television advertisers pursue them avidly.

And Trey Parker and Matt Stone, South Park's scatologically minded and sociologically astute cocreators, still know how to make them laugh. For example, they mocked the seizure of little Elian Gonzalez from his Miami relatives the very same week it happened, with an episode in which Attorney General Janet Reno, disguised as the Easter Bunny and clutching a machine gun, rescues Romanian quintuplets from Kyle, Stan, and Eric's clutches. They even satirized the ease with which child molesters find gullible children on the Web, in an episode that has chubby little Eric becoming the poster boy for the North American Man/Boy Love Association.

AT THE LEADING EDGE OF THE TWENTY-FIRST CENTURY THE SAME winds that have always buffeted television seem to be rising, perhaps pushing television's sexual content in two contradictory directions at once.

What Representative Ed Markey had predicted and lobbied for is in place: a detailed, age-based programming ratings code, modeled after the movies' ratings code, with new TV sets equipped with the governmentally mandated V-chips (for "violence"), microcircuits that give parents the ability to easily block out programming they deem objectionable—whether that objection is to violence, to language, or to sex.

In the wake of the horrifying schoolyard shootings of the late 1990s and later, leading senators and congressmen fulminate once again about the media's immorality and lack of responsibility. More hearings are held; more bills, like the Children's Defense Act and the Juvenile Justice Bill, are introduced. If only we could post the Ten Commandments in schoolrooms, some legislators thunder, and if only Hollywood stopped promoting immorality!

At least one influential legislator has raised what throughout television's history has been the ultimate specter: objectionable programming and a low moral "tone" might put individual station licenses at risk. Of course, the anti-violence rhetoric echoed the "traditional morality" themes that for decades have been raised by religious conservatives and other right wingers against programming that depicted sexual matters. Not every opponent of present-day TV is from the right, however. Liberals, leftists and centrists, from FCC Chairman Newton Minow forward, have habitually descried television's coarsening effect on American and international popular culture, as well.

In the mid-nineties, for example, the NAACP called on the Federal Communications Commission to refuse to grant Rupert Murdoch a waiver of the rule barring foreigners from owning U.S. television stations, arguing that his Fox Broadcasting network had "brought the greatest debasement of taste, character, quality and decency in television history."[44] And in the late nineties, the NAACP descried the absence of minorities on network TV, as well, leading to a mad scramble in Hollywood to bring more "people of color" into executive suites and onto program staffs.

One grassroots group even called for an annual TV Turnoff Week, so that viewers could read, get up and exercise, and reconnect with their families and communities. But, ironically, in 1999 that week began just one day after two teenagers opened fire on their classmates at Columbine High School in Littleton, Colorado. The result was to rocket TV news, news magazine, and news-related talk show ratings to their highest levels of the entire year.

Meanwhile, the conservative opponents of sexual matters on television produced a study, "Unintended Consequences: With Ratings System in Place, TV More Offensive Than Ever," that purported to demonstrate that Hollywood had used the excuse of its new, self-administered ratings code simply to increase the already shocking level of sexual content in prime-time programming. According to the 1999 study, sponsored by the Parents Television Council (PTC), a well-connected conservative "media watchdog" organization (its board of directors included Jack Valenti, head of the Motion Picture Association of America), in the two years of the age-based code's existence, nudity, profanity, and violence had risen by almost 31 percent. "Television is the raunchiest it has ever been in spite of, or perhaps because of, the ratings system," L. Brent Bozell, PTC chairman, told a U.S. congressional hearing.[45]

Sexual material on ABC, CBS, NBC, Fox, and UPN dipped slightly from 1996 to 1997, before "skyrocketing" in 1998, according to the study. The worst offender when it came to sexual content was Fox, which during the November 1998 sweeps period, averaged 7.33 sexual incidents per hour. The average among all networks was 3.5 incidents per hour.

Soon the PTC was back with another study, focusing this time on the 8 to 9 P.M. time period—the so-called family hour—and contending that 68 percent of all shows airing during that hour contained sexual material.[46]

Yet another PTC study, released after the February 2000 sweeps, claimed that TV's sexual content had tripled from 1989 to 1999, and quantified some of the increases in on-air "vulgarity" over that decade this way:

No references to oral sex in 1989, twenty a decade later. Ten to genitalia in 1989, ninety-two a decade later. Four 1989 references to homosexuality, 125 a decade later.

The organization's spokesman, with two United States senators at his side, descried TV's "decline in standards." Ironically, that spokesman was entertainer Steve Allen, who, nearly a half century before, had gotten stellar ratings by booking the young Elvis Presley on his new variety show. The result was one of the first milestones in the debate over the impact of television in the coarsening of popular culture. That debate still waxes and wanes; not surprisingly, in the presidential election year of 2000 the tide of criticism is rising once again.

With its opponents newly emboldened and with prospects so dire that lucrative TV licenses might actually be lost, Hollywood did what it always has done in periods of public concern and high

Washington dudgeon. As Peter Bart, the editor-in-chief of *Variety*, the long-time Bible of show business, put it an editorial: "While the rhetoric heats up in Washington, Hollywood proceeds as quietly as possible to make its cosmetic nips and tucks. TV episodes are canceled or shuffled around.... Development deals are stalled. Titles are softened. Everyone knows that this storm, like those before it, will blow over."

But will it?—as Bart himself asked—or was this time different, with some Rubicon finally crossed in the perpetual culture wars?

TV AFFECTS BEHAVIOR—IF AN ADVERTISER IS ASKING, BUT NOT IF a legislator wants to know.

All the tallying up of tough language and sex acts per network per hour of prime time seems somehow beside the point, unless of course you go out and survey the real world, too, which is the other half of the equation. What percentage of *your* conversation is "epithets"? How often do you and your friends make ribald remarks, talk and think about "it"?

Does TV lead society or merely follow social trends? TV people have always *wanted* to lead, but mostly only when it comes to ratings or revenue, and to beating the competition. And, of course, it's nice to win Emmys and other awards, too. But being too far ahead of society's legislators and other arbiters and moralists is not a comfortable place for a TV executive to be.

Too much sex and violence on the home screen? Well, executives say when forced to answer their many critics, TV simply reflects today's troubled world and complex social realities. Being relevant without becoming tasteless is a "difficult ball to juggle," is how one network president put it to the press in 1999.[47]

That dilemma of the network programmers is what it's always been, though this time the contradiction seems, well, more naked.

For example, NBC Entertainment President Scott Sassa began 1999 by telling the nation's assembled television critics—at the semi-annual Hollywood ritual called the Television Critics Association Press Tour—that the network needed to "tone down" the sex found in many programs. "We need to have less of an emphasis on sex," he declared. "In some cases, we use sex to get an easy laugh or sex as an easy promotional hook, and we just need to be careful with that."[48]

By late March, however, the networks were beginning to buy their new shows for the 1999–2000 season. And at NBC, one of the shows picked was *Sex Crimes*, a one-hour drama about especially heinous crimes against women and children. The new series, the network announced, would be a spin-off from its long-running and critically acclaimed *Law and Order*. And in a unique deal, *Sex Crimes* episodes would air first in prime time on NBC before moving to basic cable's USA Network one or two weeks later.

But by mid-May, "more cautious thinking" had prevailed at the then top-rated broadcast network, the only one of the original Big Three still profitable as a stand-alone operation. *Sex Crimes* was summarily retitled; henceforth, it would be known by the less provocative *Law and Order: Special Victims Unit*.

When *Special Victims* debuted that fall, it was with an episode called "Payback," focusing on the murder and sexual mutilation of a New York taxi driver. It had a cast that included Richard Belzer as John Munch, the same character he'd played in the canceled *Homicide*, and Christopher Meloni and Mariska Hargitay as detectives Stabler and Benson. Both the ratings (it was NBC's highest-rated fall drama premiere since 1995) and the reviews for the well-crafted police procedural with the torn-from-the-headlines plot were solidly favorable.

OF COURSE, THE BASIC QUESTION AT THE BEGINNING OF THE THIRD millennium is what it always has been: *Who* decides what's offensive and what's simply cutting edge?

Are sex, nudity, and raw language on serious-minded, socially engaged dramas like *NYPD Blue* or *Chicago Hope*—which, in their creators' ambitions at least, hark back to the prestigious dramatic anthologies of TV's golden age—appropriate to the subject matter and somehow more acceptable than, for example, sex, nudity, and raw language on Howard Stern or *The X Show*?

For that matter, would Dagmar have stirred less of a furor in the early fifties if her appeal had been less blatantly sexual—if she'd declaimed *meaningful* dialogue, not just doggerel, and if it were penned perhaps by Paddy Chayefsky, one of the acknowledged masters of the time? (Chayefsky, incidentally, wrote not only *Marty*, probably the most critically praised drama of TV's earliest days, but also *Network*, the prescient 1976 big-screen satire of television's anything-for-a-ratings-point ways.)

And how do the socially conservative critics of television programming protest to the advertiser today, when the advertiser is, say, Victoria's Secret and the product might be the Miracle Bra?

Civil libertarians and other critics of the critics have always said that the ultimate responsibility for home-viewing choices rests with parents, however busy and overworked. Now, for the first time the V-chip technology has made acting on that responsibility not only possible but practical. (In 2000, half of the twenty-five-million television sets sold in the United States are expected to have the microchip device. Beginning in the summer of the year, *all* TV sets with screens thirteen inches or larger will include the new technology.)

Every program on every television channel is now rated, albeit by the producers and broadcasters themselves. That ratings information is encoded in the television signal transmission, whether over the air or via cable. The V-chip then reads that encoded information and selectively blocks shows based on parents' preprogrammed criteria. ``We can't hope to be the national censor for everything that goes out over the airwaves, cable, and satellite,'' said FCC chairman William Kennard of the new device. "But [with the V-chip sets] we can empower parents."[49]

But back in the summer of 1999, as the first deadline for the new introduction of the new technology approached, even the inventor of the V-chip sounded a skeptical note, saying that public opinion polls showed that most parents thought, "I have a good handle on TV violence in my home; it's Joe next door who needs to do some work."[50]

And as the new television season took shape that summer, a suspicion grew among the social critics that, like deregulation, the new technology might not be an entirely good thing. The TV ratings system coupled with the mandatory V-chips, they feared, had given the networks greater license to push the envelope of the acceptable because viewers could block out whatever offended them.

For most of television's history, there has been more decrying of TV sex and "smut" than there was actual depiction of the same. But those days are long gone. And now that former senator and presidential candidate Bob Dole has done a TV commercial indirectly endorsing Viagra as the answer to "erectile dysfunction," even social conservatives seem prepared to talk more candidly about sex.

At the turn of the millennium, "good taste and delicacy," which once had been the solemn promise of American broadcasters, has gone on the endangered species list, nearly buffeted out of existence in the stampede by advertisers to reach teenage boys—the most coveted of all demographics—and in a public environment of scandal and sensationalism, which television can't help but transmit and amplify.

And what is it that teenage boys like to watch on television? Well, plunging necklines for one thing; hence the vogue for sword and sorcery T&A shows, such as *Xena: Warrior Princess* or *Cleopatra 2525* (from the creators of *Xena*). What had once been out of bounds, shocking, or freakish even, is now mainstream. The voyeuristic *Ugly George* cable access show had spawned *The X Show*, on FX, Fox's cable channel, which includes the occasional "sexperiment" feature, in which, for example, young women on the street are propositioned to "save the teddy bear from dismemberment" by flashing their underwear on national TV.

And Comedy Central even deems it appropriate to broadcast reruns of its *The Man Show*, which originally aired in late night, at 7 P.M. on summer Saturdays, a time when even the youngest kids might be watching. The show specializes in wriggling girls in bikinis, who fawn over the male hosts, and a typical bit would find two buxom porn stars in lingerie giving "household tips" that end with them wrestling around in a bed.

That's not exactly Howdy Doody time anymore.

OF COURSE, POLITICIANS CONTINUE TO DESCRY THE COARSENING influence of Hollywood film and TV on popular culture, just as they have since the birth of the medium. But how far will the champions of traditional "family values" go—how far *can* they go—in the new, deregulated, wired, and digitized world, even in an election year?

As anyone with even a passing knowledge of American grass-roots politics knows, as election day draws close politicos at every level resort to thumping on their Bibles, just as sheriffs running for office once became motivated to close down the local whorehouses and other pleasure palaces. With kids killing kids at Columbine and elsewhere, as the 2000 election cycle began, politicians, not surprisingly, found Hollywood a convenient and easy target.

While many Democrats were calling for stricter gun control laws, the United States Senate, dominated by conservative Republicans, geared up for the creation of a Special Committee on American Culture, to be chaired by Kansas Senator Sam Brownback, who held Hollywood responsible for creating a profane, violent, and immoral culture. For the Hollywood-based makers of popular culture the proposed committee, which would have had the power to subpoena them and their records, had all the appeal of the House Un-American Activities Committee in the fifties.

But then, when it came to taking action against Hollywood, the so-called immoralists and smut peddlers who, after all, were reliably big campaign contributors, Congress gummed the bullet instead. Within days, the erstwhile Committee on American Culture had been defanged. Democrats were insisting that guns be included in the Special Committee's mandate, so it became prudent to deny it the all-important power to issue subpoenas. It seemed prudent to give it a less ominous name, as well. So the Special Committee on American Culture, if its enabling legislation is ever actually enacted, would most likely become the Task Force on the State of American Society.[51] It would have an equal number of Republican and Democratic members and it would no longer be an instrument for a cultural inquisition.

A few months later, however, two more senators, meeting with a show business industry advocacy group, urged Hollywood film and program makers to adopt a new voluntary "code" that would lower the level of media violence and vulgarity. If the industry didn't act on its own, one of the senators warned, the more ex-

treme, uncompromising elements of society who opposed Hollywood just might.[52]

Of course, that was a veiled reference to religious fundamentalists, deeply offended by the direction of much of popular culture, who at the dawn of the new millennium continued sending
out irate press releases and organizing boycotts, just as they had
been doing for decades. Among their most prominent battles in
early 2000 were these:

- When NBC scheduled a wry little prime-time cartoon
  called *God, the Devil and Bob,* groups across the fundamentalist spectrum—from Reverend Donald Wildmon's
  American Family Association to the Council on
  American-Islamic Relations—railed against it, finding it
  tasteless and blasphemous for its depictions of God and
  the Devil battling over average guy Bob's soul. Although
  its initial ratings were strong, twenty-two of the network's
  affiliated stations refused to air it, advertisers began to
  avoid it, and after a few episodes NBC pulled it off the air.

- When HBO began promoting its *If These Wall Could
  Talk 2,* an anthology movie about three generations of
  lesbian women, Human Rights International, an organization calling itself the "world's largest pro-family, pro-life,
  pro-faith apostolate," distributed a press release entitled
  "Keep Lesbian Promotion Off Our TV Guides, or America Will Keep Your Newspapers Out of Our Homes and
  Off Our Coffee Tables!" What exercised the organization's
  president, Father Richard Welch, was not so much the TV
  movie itself, although he did call lesbianism and homosexuality "perversions," but the fact that the highly touted
  movie, which featured actresses Sharon Stone and

Ellen DeGeneres in its ensemble cast, was the cover story in many newspapers' weekly listings. "It is an attack on the American family," Father Richard declared. Nonetheless, *Walls 2* was HBO's highest rated original movie in three years.

- At about the same time as Human Rights International was denouncing televised lesbianism, the Rock for Life division of the American Life League, which calls itself the "nation's largest pro-life educational organization," was fulminating against MTV, calling it "Sex TV" and accusing it of airing shows that are "nothing more than sex/condom commercials for unwary underage teens."

- And in Utah, a state with a large, socially conservative Mormon population, the legislature passed a law creating the nation's first so-called "pornography czar"—a deputy state attorney general who will be empowered to draft new laws, investigate complaints about porn and obscenity, and prosecute offenders. However, the new law, which will have the effect of centralizing all sex-and-law issues in the state within a single office, gives the czar no authority to investigate or prosecute either cable television or the Internet. The law is not scheduled to take effect until 2001; its impact, according to legal observers, will be mostly symbolic.

BY THE MIDDLE OF THE YEAR, IN THE SAME WEEK THAT THE U.S. Supreme Court struck down a law that required cable systems to limit sexually explicit programs to late at night, and that AT&T announced that it would allow hard-core sexual programming on its cable systems, a bipartisan group of U.S. senators called on the FCC to facilitate the return of an industry-wide Code of Conduct, circumscribing "indecent" and "salacious" programming.

Meanwhile, elsewhere...

In Germany, *Baerbel*, a daytime talk show, touted an upcoming episode in which a jobless man would offer one night of sex with his wife, for one million *marks* (about half a million dollars). He'd been inspired by *Indecent Proposal*, an American movie, the man said. The real-life result was a "storm" of protest, as well as the possibility that the station could be cited as an accessory to prostitution.

Though the station rethought its plan and pulled the episode, the incident seemed a harbinger of things to come.[53]

THERE IS ONE PARTICULARLY IMPORTANT POINT TO CONSIDER about *Who Wants to Be a Millionaire,* and that is that it's an import. It originally aired in Britain, where it regularly received a remarkable seventy-plus share, and that was where it came to the attention of both William Morris agents and ABC programmers.

Once upon a time, in the earliest days of cable, broadcast network executives had warned solemnly that the big sporting events, such as the World Series, would someday no longer be available on "free" TV. That has yet to come to pass. As it's happened, though, premium "pay" TV, without advertisers to please, seems to be wooing away the best creative talents behind the best series on network television. Already, on the cusp of the new millennium, the best, most talked about comedies, TV movies, and miniseries tend to turn up on the premium pay channels.

So in the wake of *Millionaire's* stunning success on American TV, broadcast networks executives en masse combed through European TV formats for the Next Big Thing. What they found, and bet heavily on, can be summed up in a single, clinical, perhaps inevitable, word: voyeurism.

According to *Stedman's Medical Dictionary*, "voyeurism" is the practice of a) a person who derives sexual gratification from observing the naked bodies or sexual acts of others, especially from a secret vantage point; or b) an obsessive observer of sordid or sensational subjects. It is also known as "scopophilia."

Among the new, European imports that, as of this writing, American TV network executives were betting would catch fire with sensation-hungry, scopophilia-minded viewers with money to spend, are the following:

- *Survivor*, from Sweden, in which contestants are stranded on a remote island in the South Pacific and then, one by one, are voted off by the rest of the group. The last one left in this *Lord of the Flies*-like elimination takes one million dollars back to "civilization." In the original Swedish version, in what no doubt is viewed in some quarters as an unfortunate casting choice, one contestant committed suicide after being eliminated.

- *Big Brother*, from Holland, in which a group of mostly twentysomethings takes up residence in a house where their every interaction can be viewed and overheard. As in *Survivor*, which it resembles to the extent that the two shows are involved in litigation, the participants are, one by one, voted out, this time by the audience. In Europe,

Big Brother televised both sex and showers. When it comes to the bathroom and the bedroom, the CBS version drew the curtains.

- In *1900 House*, from England, a family lives in a house exactly as they would have one hundred years ago—dressing in period clothes and limited to the technology of the time, which means, among other hardships, no TV.

Of course, all three of these program "venues" will have cameras and microphones everywhere, and all are expected to have Internet elements as well, for example, allowing fans constant access to goings-on on the island or in the 1900 house.

Both *Big Brother* and *Survivor* are airing on CBS, the older-skewing erstwhile Tiffany Network, while *1900 House* airs on... PBS! Call it the apotheosis of *The Real World*, if not exactly the real world.

(Interestingly enough, it was PBS that, in 1973, broadcast *An American Family*, the forerunner of Voyeur TV. During its twelve-week run, fascinated viewers watched as the parents' marriage broke up and their son revealed that he was gay.)

Even while prognosticators and programmers were enthroning voyeurism as the Next Big Thing on network television, back at Fox a plan to crash a Boeing 747 jet in the desert (with cameras aboard, but without crew and passengers) was quickly cancelled in the face of critical scorn and a succession of unfortunately timed real-world airliner disasters that diminished the stunt's perceived entertainment value.

But not to be dissuaded, the network whose reputation for edgy comedies has been overshadowed by its reliance on disaster- and crime-video compilations, the so-called "shockumentaries," and other forms of Trash TV, came up with another sure-fire voyeuristic attention grabber for the all-important first sweeps of the year 2000.

After all, in the new Gilded Age of overnight stock-market and dot-com riches, who *wouldn't* want to marry, even sight unseen, a multimillionaire? But as it happened, there was a flaw in that casting process, too.

IT WAS A BRILLIANT IDEA—COMBINE MISS AMERICA WITH THE *Dating Game* and, in a nod to ABC's hit game show, throw in a millionaire! No, make that a *multi*millionaire!—from the very same Fox executive behind the aborted 747 smash, as well as many of the most influential shockumentary specials, including *Alien Autopsy* and *When Good Pets Go Bad*.

Fifty young women from, as they say, all walks of life competed in swimsuits, in evening gowns, and in wedding dresses, and answered questions from the titular Mr. Gotbucks (seen only in shadow until the dénouement). And at the end of the two-hour special, the dapper, tuxedoed "multimillionaire" stepped dramatically from the shadows, fell to bended knee, and proposed to the final contestant, a thirty-four-year-old emergency room nurse. Her on-air acceptance and the wedding followed immediately.

The winner of *Who Wants to Marry a Multimillionaire?*, who had to sign a prenuptial agreement, not only nabbed her multimillionaire husband, along with the two most obvious traditional accouterments (a diamond ring and an all expenses paid Caribbean "honeymoon" vacation), but got a new car, too. The ratings exceeded even the most fevered expectations—the show's final half hour captured more than one-third of all women thirty-four and younger watching TV that night; overall, Fox more than doubled its eighteen- to forty-nine-year-old adult audience over the same night a week before (when it had aired *The World's Sexiest Com-*

mercials). Plans were also unveiled *immediately* to repeat a condensed, one-hour version of the special a week later, as well as to bring a new edition of *Multimillionaire* back for the very next sweeps. But then, with soap opera suddenness: There was a twist.

First, it developed that the "multimillionaire" was also a stand-up comedian, known for his self-promoting stunts, and a veteran of the comedy·club circuit. While that in itself was no crime, soon there was a wave of appalled reaction from women's groups, critics of the medium and of popular culture, and others. "At the end of those two hours, if you turned down the volume of your TV and you listened real carefully, you could hear Western civilization crumbling around you," the director of Syracuse University's Center for the Study of Popular Television declared to the Reuters wire service. Still, even that was no crime, unless it was the crime of tastelessness which, at the dawn of the medium, broadcasters had so solemnly vowed to avoid. But that was long ago, in a world that seemed very far away. But then, a website that specialized in posting public record documents about celebrities and others reprinted the handwritten 1991 petition of a woman in Los Angeles who had filed for a temporary restraining order against Fox's putative multimillionaire, saying he had threatened to kill her when she broke off their engagement. The comic and multimillionaire "groom" denied it. But, apparently, he also had falsified elements of the biographical background information he'd given the network; there were even, as it developed, doubts about his actual net worth. The show had struck a nerve all right, but not necessarily the one its makers had intended. The damage was done.

Even as the new game show/reality hybrid trend was just beginning to accelerate, it had its first scandal. Fox's new Television Entertainment Group chairman (who had characterized the very shockumentaries the network had come to rely on as addictive "ratings crack") promptly cancelled both the *Multimillionaire's* repeat airing and its plans to mount another millionaire-marriage spectacle for the next sweeps period.

And then he even vowed to end Fox's dependence on the entire genre, canceling plans to air up to a dozen more "shock" specials, including ones called *Plastic Surgery Nightmares* and *World's Biggest Bitches.* Ironically, at least two of them—*World's Nastiest Neighbors* and *Cheating Spouses*—were snapped up immediately by UPN, Fox's competitor.

On national television less than a week later, the "bride" declared herself a Christian with pure intentions and tearfully pronounced it was all a lark gone wrong, her biggest mistake. The marriage had never been consummated, she said, and she planned to seek an annulment. And in a shrewd attempt to squeeze some lemonade from his *Multimillionaire* lemon, the Fox executive who'd created the show promptly invited the creators of The Smoking Gun, the website that had exposed the groom's past, to a meeting where they reportedly talked about the possibility of turning their popular site into a Fox show, too. But despite the *Multimillionaire* debacle, which focused a highly critical spotlight on the dangers of the game show/reality hybrid, those high ratings ensured that other producers from other studios, and from the less-constrained world of television syndication, would not be deterred. For example:

- The syndication division of one studio was working on *Wed At First Sight*, another variation of *The Dating Game.* On each episode a group of strangers would meet, compete, and, at the end of the very same episode, two of them would be married.

- Fox's own syndication division put *I Do, I Don't* into fast-track development. In it, couples about to marry submit to tests and analysis of their compatibility, as well as to a nonbinding audience vote. If the couple decides to proceed, the wedding takes place at the end of the very same episode.

- Another syndication company is offering *Cheaters*, in which hidden cameras will try to catch unfaithful spouses in the act. The straying spouse will then be confronted by their cuckolded partner, while cameras roll.

Whether or not shows like this will be successful, or even if they will actually make it on the air is, as of this writing, not yet known. However, the fact that early episodes of *Survivor* topped *Millionaire* with those coveted young audiences makes it much more likely the genre will thrive. But what's clear, even to someone without a crystal ball, is that this time it's not just Christian fundamentalists and "family value" zealots who are appalled.

WOULD ALLEN FUNT, THE AVUNCULAR CREATOR OF *CANDID Camera,* that innocent precursor to today's voyeuristic reality and game shows be surprised at the sexy explicitness and high titillation quotient of television's hottest "new" genre? Not hardly! The evidence that Funt himself anticipated the newest New Thing by three decades is probably right there in the adult section of your local video store: *What Do You Say to a Naked Lady?,* written and directed by Funt himself, was as good-natured and funny as *Camera,* but when it was released on the big screen in 1970 it was with an adults-only "X" rating. The gags were sexy and included full-frontal nudity, such as the bit in which a hidden camera catches the shock and amazement on the faces of everyday folks innocently awaiting an elevator at the exact instant the door whooshes open and a completely nude young woman marches out.

OF COURSE, THERE ARE ANY NUMBER OF UPSCALE "VIEWERS" for whom TV voyeurism is not some shocking new departure, and among them are the online aficionados of sexually explicit video streaming on the Internet. Take, for example, voyeur-dorm.com and its imitators.

Voyeurdorm is an adults-only website where round-the-clock cameras track a group of coeds living in a house in Tampa, Florida. Wherever they go in the house, whatever they do there, is just a mouse click away. Of course, the new reality game hybrids, all of which are expected to provide video streaming at their affiliated websites, will be voyeurdorm's latest competitors. Call it another example of convergence. "Convergence," the most fraught buzzword of the media's digital transition, refers to both the technology of TV and its content, to both the hardware and the software.

Soon, say the evangelists of convergence, speaking of a "television set" and a "computer" will be anachronistic. Soon, there will be no distinction at all between your TV set and your computer, between your telephone and your cable converter box; all data, from e-mail to the latest pay-per-view Hollywood blockbuster, will arrive through the same fiber optic cable and will be displayed on the same flat, high-definition screen. It will be one seamless web of WebTV. And then what?

Will networks go away? Will movie theaters disappear? Remember, as far back as the early fifties, the advent of television prompted dire predictions that the end of the movies and of radio was coming.

Similarly, in the era of the media mega-merger (AOL/Time-Warner, pending as of this writing; Viacom/CBS; GE/NBC; Disney/ABC; News Corp./Fox; and so on) and worldwide vertical integration, "product" is converging, too, and a rush to occupy bandwidth on the web is one of the forms that convergence is taking.

The sexiness of the new medium is a singular attraction for established TV talent: even more than cable, it's uncut, uncensored, and raw. Early examples of the new trend:

- The creators of *South Park* are making animated shorts for the Web

- The creators of HBO's voyeuristic *Taxicab Confessions* are launching a site that specializes in hidden webcams

- National Lampoon is producing a new animated series on its website. *Flush Life*, as it's called, will follow the adventures of public-bathroom graffiti that comes to life.

Someday perhaps, we'll all be treated to the adults-only web adventures of Tinky Winky, the gay Teletubby, too. Well, not really. But, in 1999, the Reverend Jerry Falwell did create something less than a furor—there was too much derisive laughter for that— when he charged that Tinky Winky was a covert gay role model.

Convergence is beginning to go in the other direction, too (and not just in the early 2000 deal that shocked Hollywood, the proposed acquisition of Time Warner by America Online), and of course sex and sexiness is leading the way: Cindy Margolis, the self-styled "most downloaded woman on the Internet," is getting her own one-hour talk and variety show, which will air from Miami's South Beach. The series will be produced by King World, the same syndication powerhouse behind *Oprah, Jeopardy,* and *Wheel of Fortune*, which, in still another example of how the media world is converging, was recently purchased by CBS, which in turn has been acquired by Viacom.

So let's not even call it simply "television" anymore—the word itself is beginning to sound so, well, retro and fifties. The plunging necklines of the fifties have evolved into Jennifer Lopez's barely-there Versace dress at the 2000 Grammys. Rob and Laura in separate beds have morphed into Sharon and Ellen, as a gay couple in a prestigious cable movie, playing artificial insemination for gentle laughs.

Where is all this heading? Whither the "home medium"? The social critics will continue to argue that we've traded tastefulness in our living rooms for crass sensationalism and worse. And in a world where sex shows—for example, *Live From Tijuana!*—on our home screens are not only possible, they're interactive and always available, there's an obvious truth to that. But it's at least equally the case that we've sacrificed the dubious notion of "taste" for greater variety, more candor, and less hypocrisy.

Will there soon be nothing you can't say on the home screen, even on over-the-air broadcasts, at least while employing the convenient fiction of the electronic bleep?

Are we moving inexorably toward a less sexually repressed society, too, perhaps even toward something that might be called the libertine society, where nothing sexual that is consenting is too kinky to end up showing whenever we want to see it, right here in the living room, on our new digital, broadband, high-definition, in-house entertainment and information center? Or is all this just another swing of the social pendulum, farther out than before, but merely awaiting some new outrage or scandal—and Voyeur TV and whatever follows it will offer abundant opportunities for just that—to brake and come crashing back?

That's for later to decide.

Los Angeles, California
June 2000

Afterword

To those of you who find my meandering and digressive history of TV sex and its highlights idiosyncratic or incomplete; who wonder why so little Maggie and Joel (after all I wrote the book about that one); or ask whatever happened to the babes on *Baywatch*, or to Palladin's San Francisco courtesans; or who ask, where's that awesomely mystical erotic moment in *Kung Fu*, or that phasers-on-stunningly-sexy *Space: Above and Beyond* hooker scene ("You can do anything but kiss me") set aboard the pleasure ship *Bacchus*, a military brothel in outer space; and how come not a word about *Drew Carey, The Kids in the Hall*, or Rowan Atkinson's sublimely suggestive *Black Adder*? To you I say:

Gentle reader, if you think you can do better, you're welcome to try. Send your suggestions and comments, querulous or otherwise, directly to me at LChunovic@aol.com or in care of the publisher, TV Books, 1619 Broadway, 9th floor, New York, N.Y. 10019.

I'll be pleased to incorporate your best ideas into any future edition of this book.

Citations

1. *Time*, October 29, 1951.
2. *Los Angeles Times*, September 19, 1999.
3. *Business Week*, November 23, 1951.
4. *Saturday Evening Post*, December 27, 1952.
5. *Time*, July 9, 1951.
6. *Newsweek*, December 11, 1950.
7. *The Book of TV Lists,* by Gabe Essoe (Arlington House, 1981), p. 69.
8. *Saturday Evening Post*, December 27, 1952.
9. Ibid.
10. *Los Angeles Mirror*, May 27, 1953.
11. *Los Angeles Mirror*, April 23, 1951.
12. Ibid.
13. Ibid.
14. *The "I Love Lucy" Book*, by Bart Andrews (Doubleday, 1985), pp. 98, 102.
15. *Newsweek*, November 17, 1955.
16. *Saturday Review*, November 17, 1956.
17. *Los Angeles Mirror*, January 22, 1954.
18. *Last Train to Memphis: The Rise of Elvis Presley*, by Peter Guralnick (Back Bay Books, 1994), p. 519.
19. Ibid. p. 379.
20. *The Century*, ABC News, April 5, 1999.
21. *Los Angeles Mirror*, October 17, 1959.
22. *Variety*, December 14, 1999.
23. *Time*, April 8, 1966.

24. Ibid.

25. *America*, December 2, 1967.

26. *Los Angeles Herald-Examiner,* April 24, 1969.

27. *Los Angeles Herald-Examiner TV Weekly*, June 15–21, 1969.

28. *The Book of TV Lists,* by Gabe Essoe (Arlington House, 1981), pp. 66–67.

29. *Variety*, December 2, 1999.

30. *Newsweek*, June 15, 1981.

31. *U.S. News & World Report,* June 8, 1992.

32. *Psychology Today*, September/October 1992.

33. *Los Angeles Times*, May 9, 1999.

34. From an account in the *New Yorker*, August 16, 1993.

35. *TV Guide*, April 4–10, 1992.

36. *Nightline*, June 15, 1999.

37. The *X-Files* episode entitled "Mind's Eye."

38. *New York Times*, April 5, 1998.

39. *New York Times*, July 19, 1999.

40. *U.S. News & World Report*, September 11, 1995.

41. *New York Times*, March 18, 1999.

42. As reported by KTLA-TV, Los Angeles, on its 10:00 P.M. newscast, February 17, 2000.

43. *New York Times*, August 28, 1999.

44. Reuters, May 27, 1999.

45. *Variety*, September 1, 1999.

46. *Variety*, June 13, 1999.

47. Reuters, August 1, 1999.

48. *UltimateTV* (online), January 1, 1999.

49. *Variety*, June 10, 1999.

50. *Los Angeles Times*, June 30, 1999.

51. *Variety*, September 24, 1999.

52. Reuters, January 31, 1999.

53. Reuters, January 26, 2000.

Index

About the Author

Louis Chunovic is the former television editor of the *Hollywood Reporter* newspaper, the former managing editor of *Variety's On Production* magazine, and the former on-air entertainment reporter for Fox Television in Los Angeles.

His books include *Bruce Lee: The Tao of the Dragon Warrior; The Rocky and Bullwinkle Book; Jodie: A Biography; Northern Exposure: The Book; Quantum Leap: The Book; The Caroline in the City Companion; Marilyn Monroe at Twentieth Century Fox*, by Lawrence Crown (a pseudonym); and the novels *Hyde and Seek* and *Hyde in Deep Cover*, both by Benjamin Wolff (a pseudonym).

He is also the author of a privately printed history of the Hollywood Radio and Television Society, commissioned on the occasion of that organization's fiftieth anniversary.

Other publications for which he has written include the *Advocate, American Film, Entertainment Weekly*, the *Fort Lauderdale Sun-Sentinel*, the *Journal of the Writers Guild of America*, the *Las Vegas Sun*, the *Los Angeles Times, Movieline, PC World, Pulse*, the *Saint*

Paul Pioneer Press, the *San Francisco Examiner, Screen* magazine, *TV Guide, Us, Weekly Variety,* and others.

He has recently completed a novel, set in Hollywood, about the TV business and television news.